the WELL-ORGANIZED HOME

RYLAND
PETERS
& SMALL

LONDON NEW YORK

the WELL-ORGANIZED HOME

hard-working storage solutions for every room in the house

Judith Wilson

First published in the United Kingdom
in 2005 by

Ryland Peters & Small
20–21 Jockey's Fields
London WC1R 4BW
www.rylandpeters.com

10 9 8 7 6 5 4 3 2 1

ISBN 1 84172 935 3

A CIP record for this book is available
from the British Library.

Printed and bound in China.

Senior Editor **Clare Double**
Location Research **Emily Westlake**
Production **Gavin Bradshaw**

Art Director **Gabriella Le Grazie**
Publishing Director **Alison Starling**

CONTENTS

INTRODUCTION

OPPOSITE AND ABOVE: **We all live busy lives, so creating an organized infrastructure at home makes it easier to find things in a hurry. Open shelves are the perfect solution for instant, see-at-a-glance access. Don't be embarrassed to plan them in minute detail. What works for you? Books may be grouped in subject or alphabetical order, files or papers clustered into transparent holders or boxes, and even clothes can be colour-coded. Shelves, box files or containers can also be labelled for extra clarity.**

there's a palpable tranquillity to the well-organized home. We may not register quite how – or why – good storage affects us. Yet a lack of visual clutter, combined with order behind cupboard doors, goes a long way towards encouraging relaxed living. If the entire household knows where to find key items – and, by definition, where to tidy them away – home runs on well-oiled wheels.

Whether you're a minimalist, or after simple elegance, great storage is also the key to a good-looking, streamlined home. These days, that has never been more important. The clean spaces we favour today have demanded a sea change in storage. Once, classic free-standing pieces and occasional built-in shelves were the norm. Now, storage must be capacious and discreet – specifically to keep daily ephemera at bay – and is often woven into the fabric of the home. It may be expected to make a design statement or, in open-plan zones, to divide living spaces, too.

Our relationship with the very things we store has also changed. In our consumer-driven society, most households are bursting with more possessions than ever. On the other hand, influenced by minimalism, there's pressure to sort your stuff and recycle. We also have different things to store: more technology and gadgets, but less paperwork, as photos, music and documents are swallowed up into the computer.

So it's vital to keep abreast of our storage needs and find out what works now. Keeping a beady eye on what comes into the house (where will it live? what should go to make room?) is a great habit to cultivate, as is having a regular clear-out of clothes, children's handiwork and so on. Often, we plan extra storage because we feel we're drowning in clutter. Sometimes, the answer lies in getting rid of extraneous stuff and reorganizing – rather than adding to – the storage we already have.

REVIEWING EXISTING STORAGE

Whether you're moving into a new home or revamping the one you have, it's always sensible to start with an overview of the storage in place. Walk around every room and make notes. What pieces function efficiently and are easy to keep tidy, and why? What actively motivates you, and/or other family members, to use these systems properly?

ABOVE: **Don't overlook odd-shaped spaces, as they can very usefully accommodate infrequently used items such as out-of-season clothes. With their sloping ceilings, the under-eaves spaces found in loft conversions can be fitted with low-level shelf units, or inexpensive stacking plastic crates. Add good lighting, so it's easy to find things, and ensure the space is well-insulated and dry before storing precious items.**

RIGHT: **Design storage to get the best out of odd 'spare' areas. In this narrow hall, shallow open shoe racks, fitted floor to ceiling, take up less space than a conventional cupboard.**

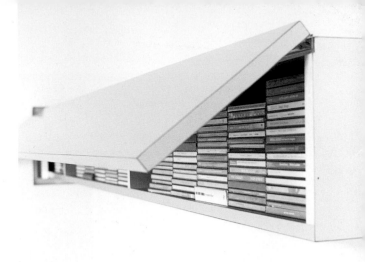

Which storage looks good visually? Does it enhance the look of the room, and does its internal arrangement please you? Is the amount, and type, of storage appropriate to the room in which it is located?

Equally, take note of what storage doesn't seem to work. Is there simply not enough of it, or is it badly organized? Are your cupboards user-friendly but located in an awkward area? Are shelves or cupboards in good condition, but looking out of date? In this case, it's always possible to adapt the existing carcass with alternative trims or fresh doors. Also identify any places where clutter builds up, a sure sign that extra capacity is needed. Look around the house to evaluate potential new storage areas such as alcoves, 'dead' landing space or quirky recesses. Finally, ask yourself what specialist storage you long for. It's amazing how a customized shoe rack or neatly planned home library can truly improve the quality of daily life!

In tandem with the review, compile detailed lists of everything you have to store. Consider this room by room, over time, so the task doesn't seem too daunting: there are checklists at the end of each chapter to get you started. You'll soon reap the benefits. There's nothing like looking in every cupboard to help weed out unnecessary clutter and – if you're intimately acquainted with how many shoes/CDs/magazines you own – designing and measuring up for storage is a breeze.

TOP RIGHT: **An overview of existing storage can prompt unusual new ideas, and make you reassess less obvious places for adding more. Slim, custom-built units at eye level or skirting height will squeeze extra square centimetres out of a small space with a restricted floor area. Equally, take advantage of particularly lofty proportions. This room** (RIGHT) **looks very dramatic with bookshelves stretching up to the ceiling.**

FAR RIGHT: **If you're adding to existing cupboards, it's not always essential to build matching units. The addition of a shop-bought trolley or unit on wheels can improve storage no end.**

LEFT: In a high-traffic family room, casual open-shelf storage is the best option for an assortment of books, DVDs and magazines. A grid arrangement will lend the illusion of neatness, even if volumes aren't stacked in perfect order. Providing plenty of shelves, as in this floor-to-ceiling design, keeps the floor clear of clutter.

THIS PICTURE: Even if space doesn't permit a separate office, those working from home will need a designated shelf unit or cupboard to keep private papers together. Picking office-style, clearly labelled storage boxes and files sends a clear message to everyone else that this is a working zone.

LIFESTYLE CONSIDERATIONS

Just as each of us has a unique character, we all have an individual way of life at home. It pays to examine that. While our daily clothes should match our lifestyle, so also our storage needs to be closely tailored to the ways we like to live at home. First, think through your storage 'personality'. If you like to exist in lightly organized chaos, then it makes sense to plan for casual, easy-access shelves and hooks requiring minimum effort. Tidiness freaks, however, will be better off with carefully planned drawers and shelves, concealed behind doors. Be honest with yourself. There's no point choosing a grid of open shelves, fitted with lidded boxes, if you can't be bothered to keep them tidy.

The number of people at home, the amount of time they spend there and what they do, also affects organization. A working couple out of the house all day will require streamlined systems that aid a quick getaway in the mornings, and minimal tidying up. In a family home, by contrast, varied storage options must allow for easy toy access for children, space for bikes and sports kit, and quick-tidy options (such as baskets and hooks) for a painless clear-up at night. Those who work from home, or pursue an active hobby, may need specialized storage, housed in a home office or exterior studio. Observe the house at the end of a busy day. What are the problem areas? Where has stuff accumulated?

However well planned and capacious, storage systems will only work like clockwork if everyone in the household is motivated to use them. So think through the storage personalities of other family members, too. Children can be encouraged to tidy up if storage is suitably tailored to them, such as floor-level crates or low coat hooks. Teenagers will be inclined to keep their own spaces tidy if provided with cool, industrial-style shelving and a hanging rack, rather than a conventional wardrobe. And there's nothing wrong with a few house rules. Tell everyone to hang up coats on arrival home, put back DVDs after use, and sort the recycling.

Any household will also benefit from a twice-yearly seasonal shift in possessions to keep things moving smoothly. Just as you don't want outdoor clothes cluttering a utility room in summer, out-of-season kit like deckchairs can be stowed in winter. Plan your home with seasonal storage in mind: a loft, dry cellar or top cupboards are all good options.

ABOVE: **A family kitchen should be cleverly planned so that everyone can help with unloading the dishwasher and keeping things tidy. Open shelves, with casual stacks of plates and cups, leave no excuses.**

FAR LEFT: **In an open-plan space that must cope with several activities, from cooking to kids playing, storage can be a useful way to define the different zones. In this industrial, modern sitting room, the slim bookshelf takes up minimal space, yet neatly holds all the children's books close to the play area. The top levels hold art and reference books.**

ABOVE: **If you are devoting an entire wall to cupboards, plan the style and materials as carefully as you might a wallpaper or fabric. To make flush floor-to-ceiling cupboards 'disappear', paint MDF doors in a colour to match the walls. If choosing timber or veneer doors, ask to see a large sample in order to gauge the overall effect, as highly decorative grains can look very dominant.**

RIGHT: **Check out unusual sources to give a fresh twist to purpose-built shelving. These riveted steel units, originally destined as warehouse shelving, add a raw decorative contrast to the sleek wood finishes.**

LEFT: **Take time to research good containers to line up on shelves or over wall cupboards. As well as the high street, look at mail-order storage catalogues and office-supply stores. Match the container to the mood in the room. For a simple country finish, woven baskets or timber containers look great, or for a wackier storage option try glass cube vases or identical sturdy brown carrier bags.**

DECIDING ON A STYLE

In today's style-conscious times, it is vital to plan storage that is as smart as it is practical. Take time to choose looks and finishes that appeal. As well as leafing through interiors magazines, visit home stores to look at designer storage systems and check out high-street shops for budget options that may be customized. Do your research in less obvious places, too. Look carefully at the ways shops display goods, as shop fittings are often imaginatively designed. In restaurants, check out how they stack tableware, combining ease of access with good looks.

Early on, decide whether cupboards and shelves will blend with the interior architecture at home. In a period property, with pretty panelling or high skirting boards, it makes sense to match built-in joinery to the prevailing style. In small rooms, such uniformity will also enhance the space. But in a large room or an open-plan zone, it can be fun to use storage to set a new decorative tone. The more you find out about potential surfaces for doors, or shelf trims, the more imaginative the looks will be. As well as rich timber veneer, stainless steel or painted MDF, you could consider frosted glass, perspex, and fabric or suede.

Detailing matters too, so look for decorative handles for cupboards and drawers. There's a huge range, from stainless steel to resin, glass to leather: often, just adding new handles can instantly update storage. If open shelves are to be lined with containers, choose wisely. Identical wicker baskets, zinc tubs or perspex boxes look smart lined up, but buy a few spares, so that you can add gradually to the storage system.

LONG-TERM PLANNING

Given its key role at home, storage deserves to be minutely planned and beautifully built, but too often it is an afterthought. We're more likely to spend funds on an eye-catching sofa. But allocating a generous budget to bespoke cupboards and drawers brings rewards. Well-built storage withstands much wear and tear, and is a strong selling point when you move. Thoughtfully planned, with a strong visual theme, cohesive storage is also the ideal way to give your home individual style.

Whenever possible, plan storage across the whole home, rather than rooms in isolation. This way, you can organize possessions according to activity and frequency of use, rather than being constrained by room functions. For example, instead of every child keeping toys in their room, a wall of toy cupboards in the kitchen would free space for individual desk areas. Rather than having assorted TVs at home, allocate one small room as a media zone, with storage for DVDs and equipment. Once you've zoned storage in the appropriate places, it's easy to spot any spare space, and use that for housing out-of-season paraphernalia.

Allow for flexibility when planning. Collections always grow, so plan new storage with room to spare. Design systems with dual potential: shelving for a home office, for example, might later become spare-room clothes storage. And don't forget that you can hire a storage unit. A year on, when you haven't missed a single item, ebay will be your first stop.

LEFT: **Many people baulk at the cost of buying quality, smart containers, but they really are a worthwhile investment. Even if you move house, they can be freshly labelled and adapted to a new set of shelves. Take the same view when buying traditionally unseen containers, such as wedding-dress storage boxes, suit bags or multiple perspex shoeboxes. Buying them may not be as exciting as choosing a designer vase, but they will certainly protect your clothes from dust and moths.**

LEFT AND ABOVE: **You should always spend as much as you can afford on great storage, but make choices according to how long you intend to stay at a given property. If you're doing up a budget flat, insist on quality craftsmanship, but stick with economical finishes. A long-term home, by contrast, deserves beautiful materials like wood or leather, which will improve over time. Serial house-movers should spend money on a quirky free-standing piece, which can be moved when you do.**

KITCHENS

ASSESSING SPACE AND LIFESTYLE

The kitchen is the hardest-working space in the home. We expect to cook and store food in it, house tableware and equipment there, as well as use it for eating and socializing. Yet despite this consistently high level of activity, we often neglect kitchen planning, preferring to focus on good looks. But great storage is vital. If there's a place for everything, the kitchen – however tiny – looks more streamlined. A well-ordered environment also guarantees a safe and efficient zone, as practical as it is welcoming.

First, assess the available space. Review existing storage and whether it works well, and consider if there's room to add more cupboards. If the kitchen is really tiny, and building work is an option, consider extending the space, either by knocking through into an adjacent room or adding a garden extension. If you are stuck with small dimensions, consider any other space-saving potential. In a room with high ceilings, storage may be maximized by double-height wall cupboards. 'Spare' fireplace alcoves may be filled in with flush cupboards.

ABOVE LEFT: **The decorative look you choose will directly affect the amount, and type, of storage. The strict minimalism here, for example, requires plenty of cupboards, so everyday items are stored away with just a few well-chosen accessories left out on show.**

ABOVE RIGHT: **In a more relaxed kitchen-dining room, divided by an island, storage should be planned so it may be easily accessed from both sides. This unit, fitted with drawers and cupboards, looks sleek yet is very user-friendly.**

RIGHT: **In a busy cook's kitchen, pick a casual style so that pans and jars are stored in full view and remain easily to hand.**

Your lifestyle, and the number of people using the kitchen, must also come into the equation. For a single person, a galley kitchen may suffice. By contrast, a family kitchen – which may also double as a playroom and sitting room – needs quantities of clever storage, tailored to cope with everything from toys to tableware. Think through a day in the life of your projected kitchen, and focus on practical needs. What mood and look are you hoping for? A penchant for minimalist splendour, or a casual look, will radically affect the type of storage you need.

LEFT: **There isn't always the luxury to devote an entire room to the kitchen. In an open-plan loft or studio flat, you may need to conceal the working kitchen itself, so that it doesn't jar with a sitting/dining area. This calls for careful planning. First, there will be space constraints. You will need to balance possible lack of wall space for cupboards against the need for good storage, so the area remains streamlined. Second, you may need to plan an additional layer of doors, so the working kitchen may be concealed. In this tiny kitchen zone, cupboards are stacked vertically, to maximize a high ceiling, and any clutter hidden behind a sliding door.**

WHAT NEEDS STORING?

First use the checklists at the end of the chapter to kick-start a personalized list of what needs storing. Once you have the basics on paper – foodstuffs, cooking equipment, tableware and so on – you can begin to categorize items to provide the most user-friendly arrangement. Don't forget to include extras such as a radio or cookery books, which may be just as much a part of kitchen life as the kettle.

Given that most of us eat in the kitchen, you'll need plenty of space for tableware, cutlery and assorted extras such as serving plates. If eating areas are split into a formal table and a breakfast bar, it may help to divide 'best' tableware and everyday items, siting them in separate areas close to each zone. By contrast, all key equipment, from pans to blender, must go in the cooking area. Think about small electrical appliances. The coffee maker and toaster should be immediately accessible: rarely used gadgets such as an ice-cream maker can be stored.

Food storage requires special attention. You need room in the fridge, vegetable baskets and bread bin for fresh foods, plus plenty of cupboard space for dry goods. As well as grouping like with like – oils and spices, pastas and rice – consider arranging foods according to weight (with heavy items stored low) or height (such as tall cereal packets or bottles of oil).

Finally, check all categories, and concentrate all daily essentials – from food to gadgets – in the most convenient places. It's your style choice whether they are in cupboards, on the worktop or hanging up. What matters most is that they are located between waist height and eye level, to avoid constant bending. Allocate remaining top cupboards or low drawers for infrequently used things like picnicware.

ABOVE: **Cooking implements are best located right next to the hob. For efficiency, fix a long steel rail to the splashback, and hang a matching set from individual butcher's hooks. If drawer space is lacking, a cutlery basket can organize knives and forks.**

LEFT: **Dry foodstuffs should be kept fresh in well-sealed jars. Glass jars, lined en masse along a shelf or worktop, provide a decorative and practical display.**

ABOVE: There's an art to stacking tableware. Nestle serving bowls one inside another, but locate them on a low shelf so access is easy. Try to keep plates and bowls in individual piles, so you don't constantly have to shift one stack to get to another.

INSET: Cookery books and small appliances need to be out on show, but they clutter a worktop. Keep them neat in a built-in niche.

RIGHT: Crockery is most efficient piled only one layer deep in shallow cupboards. If building new storage, measure the biggest plates for depth.

VARYING YOUR OPTIONS

Given the vast array of items to be accommodated, the best kitchens offer a good mix of options. Your choices will be dictated largely by the style of kitchen you want and your storage 'personality'. But do some research, too, to see which combinations most appeal. It may be tempting to go for a purist visual option – perhaps a bank of flush cupboards – but good looks must be combined with practicality.

The cupboard is the most conventional kitchen choice, but they've moved on from just the wall or under-worktop varieties. Most kitchen companies also offer floor-to-ceiling cupboards, shallow eye-level units and tiered units. In addition to size, consider the available types of door – double, single, flap-up or -down, shuttered – and the internal layout.

Drawers are invaluable for cutlery, linen and foils. Shallow variants are good for organizing small items such as cake decorations, while medium ones – fitted with plate organizers – can even hold stacked crockery. Deep drawers, preferably below the hob, are perfect for pans. Specialist options include wicker or wire drawers for storing vegetables.

Open shelves offer easy access to kitchen kit, but can be high-maintenance. Be prepared to dust regularly. Wall-mounted shelves at eye level need to be kept particularly tidy. By contrast, deep shelves tucked below a worktop can be stacked with small appliances or pans, and still look acceptable. When choosing, consider all potential shelf materials – steel, wood, glass, MDF – as well as ensuring that the shelves can be well secured to the wall.

Don't forget specialist storage options, including swing-out units that utilize corner space, larder units with pull-out baskets, built-in wine racks and more.

ABOVE: **Open shelves tucked beneath a worktop give the best of both worlds: items are protected from dust, while being easy to access. The worktop also provides useful display space, keeping cooking space free.**

RIGHT: **In a narrow space, a bank of drawers, rather than cupboards, can be a space-saving solution.**

OPPOSITE: **Designing a kitchen, and having a joiner build it, is the best way to get truly customized storage. This robust arrangement, blending open steel shelves, hanging options and tiered containers, combines practicality with industrial-style chic.**

TOP AND RIGHT: **Don't ruin the flush finishes of a fitted kitchen by adding fussy detailing. Cupboards should sport minimal handles or touch-catch fittings. Keep splashbacks between wall and base units simple, with glass, stainless-steel or painted surfaces rather than tiles.**

ABOVE: **A mix-and-match free-standing kitchen still needs uniformity. By painting the dresser and the built-in shelf unit white, this owner has neatly drawn the look together.**

ABOVE FAR RIGHT: **Table-style sink units blend easily with casual, unfitted storage. Also look out for industrial-style kitchen worktops, conveniently fitted with appliances but with a free-standing look.**

For those after a more relaxed look, consider mixing a large free-standing piece such as a traditional dresser, sideboard or serving table with drawers, with built-in shelves and free-standing appliances. Visually, such furniture gives the kitchen 'room' appeal, while still offering practical storage. Key pieces can be teamed with mobile furniture such as a butcher's block, metal catering trolley on wheels, or a trestle table. Not everyone wants to hunt junk shops for appropriate pieces. If you want the practicality of purpose-built units, but a flexible layout, check out free-standing-style kitchen ranges: the high street has some excellent variations.

BUILT-IN VERSUS FREE-STANDING

There's an enduring appeal to the built-in kitchen. Banks of cupboards look sleek, conceal clutter and can be tailored to find a home for anything, even the ironing board. You can also have the practicality of drawers and shelves, but cover them up with flush cupboards. Fitted cupboards can stretch from floor to ceiling, maximizing wall space if floor area is in short supply, or be built across awkward alcoves for a uniform finish. Use recommendations to find a good fitted-kitchen specialist (some companies don't offer quite the bespoke service they promise), or hire a joiner to build to your own design.

Visually, do try to avoid overpowering banks of wall and base units, especially if they are on two or more walls. These days, the most modern option is to combine a full wall of cupboards with an island unit, or create a galley-style run of units just down one wall. Once you've sorted the internal layout, major decisions will concern door styles. Whether you pick painted MDF, lacquer, sand-blasted glass, stainless steel or timber, remember that the surface will set the decorative tone in the room.

BELOW: **If you need to build in units to get the most out of a small space, yet still want a free-standing mood, combine fitted base cupboards with casual storage such as a ceiling pan store and wall-mounted plate rack.**

ISLAND UNITS

Island units act as a work zone and a breakfast bar, not to mention being a sociable focal point. They are also rich in storage potential. Before planning one, check there's sufficient floor area. You'll need one metre of circulation space all round, plus enough worktop overhang for tucking in stools. An island unit can be square, rectangular or even round, though bespoke curved cupboard doors will cost more. An extension of the island concept is a longer, industrial-style work bench, which may be teamed with a wall of cupboards for a free-standing look.

The type of storage you incorporate depends on the function of the island. If it's to be the cooking zone, with built-in gas hob and oven, then pan

ABOVE: **If there's only enough space for an island unit with cupboards on one side, there may be room on the reverse to insert a narrow storage niche. This one is fitted with a built-in wine rack.**

RIGHT: **Properly planned, an island unit should have a place for everything, so that the worktops can remain clutter-free.**

RIGHT: In this minimalist kitchen, the island unit has been teamed with a recessed cupboard at one end of the room and a generous bank of drawers. Sliding doors complete the streamlined look.

BELOW: A large island unit will be the centre of attention in an open-plan space. Brightly painted open shelves combine storage and display space.

drawers and open shelves for oils and spices will be the order of the day. If it's a breakfast bar, plan flush cupboards for tableware and cereals. Positioning is crucial. If stools flank one side, install storage at one or both ends instead. How wide will the island be? Decide whether to include shallow cupboards on either side, or deep shelves accessed from one side only. Think about traffic flow around the island.

Where space is tight, sliding doors or open shelves will be less obtrusive than hinged doors.

In a multi-functional kitchen, in which the island divides cooking and eating/play zones, vary storage options on alternate sides. Add doors on the kitchen side to match wall units, and on the opposite side add a mix of open shelves and drawers. Low-level storage like this is great for toys and books.

DISPLAY STORAGE

We've become so used to streamlined kitchens that everyday domestic ephemera, from fruit bowls to coffee cups, have all but disappeared from view. Yet such items bring immense personality to the kitchen. Unless you're committed to minimalism proper, plan at least some storage that doubles as a decorative display. It's not enough to fill shelves with an odd assortment of items. Actively plan the design with your thoughts on what will be displayed, and how.

Display storage works best within a confined space, to focus the eye and restrict the number of objects. Look for natural alcoves, which may be lined with shelves, in an existing kitchen, or plan to add a shelf unit to break up a run of cupboards. If you're doing building work, consider sinking one or

ABOVE: **You can't beat the appeal of varied foodstuffs in jars, especially glass. Look for jars with an efficient seal, in a style that matches the kitchen. For a modern look, choose cubed glass or stainless-steel styles. In a country kitchen, choose enamel or tin, perhaps with pretty lettering, or amass a varied collection of antique glass preserving jars.**

OPPOSITE, BELOW LEFT: **In this busy, cook's kitchen, all everyday essentials are on show, stacked on an open grid of shelving. There's an honest charm about the mix of ordinary food packaging and simple tableware, but it will also help to keep an eye out for especially pretty labelling on jars or packets.**

OPPOSITE, RIGHT: **Despite the apparently haphazard mix of items here, they have all been carefully chosen to please the eye. The plain cellophane and brown paper packaging, retro teapot and radio, and casually stacked linens fill the shelves nicely and look cohesive.**

ABOVE LEFT: **Even if tableware and food are stored behind closed doors, no one wants to open them on chaos. Take time to plan cupboard interiors. Despite being fully stacked, this one is still neatly organized, with a place for everything. If the height of shelves permits, you might include cup hooks below shelves, to make mugs easier to access. Give as much decorative consideration to the insides of the cupboards as the exterior. Paint them a darker, contrast colour, or line shelves with patterned oilcloth.**

ABOVE RIGHT: **Carefully placed wall-hung storage can add character and a splash of colour to a simple kitchen.**

more niches into a false plasterboard wall. Vary built-in shelving, particularly above a worktop, by using a grid design, which helps to organize items and also looks good. In a country-style kitchen, consider adding junk-shop finds: a plate rack or quirky painted wood shelves are excellent choices.

As well as placing frequently used objects, such as a teapot or radio, in accessible spots, arrange everyday items with an eye for decorative potential. Line up foodstuffs in identical jars, sort cookery books by size or colour or stack steel cookware attractively. Then consider ways to highlight the display. In a modern kitchen, inset low-voltage lights to illuminate recessed shelves. More traditionally, paint the shelf interiors a contrast colour to highlight the contents.

KITCHEN CHECKLISTS

ITEMS TO ACCOMMODATE

EQUIPMENT
Pans and cooking dishes

Knives, cutlery, implements

Coffee machine, juicer, blender

Toaster

Microwave

Baking kit

Picnic kit, Thermos, kids'
   lunchboxes

TABLEWARE
Cutlery

Plates, cups, glasses, etc.

Table linen

Tea towels, foil, sandwich
   bags, etc.

Candles, big dishes, etc.

Fruitbowls

Jugs

FOODSTUFFS
Dry foods

Fresh vegetables and fruit

Tins, bottles, jars of food

Jars of tea, coffee, sugar, etc.

Bread, bread bin

DOMESTIC ITEMS
Cleaning cloths, liquids
   and sprays

Bucket, dustpan and brush

Washing-up brush, liquid
   soap, etc.

OTHER ITEMS
Flower vases

Hi-fi/radio and music

Computer

Cookery books

Pens and paper

ISSUES TO ADDRESS

- Do you need to accommodate a dining table and chairs within the kitchen and, if so, where will the tableware be stored?
- What mood are you trying to convey – casual, formal, sociable or a mix of all three?
- What's the budget?
- How flexible can you be on changing the space you have – is there the option to knock together two rooms or add an extension?
- Do you like a minimal, everything-put-away look, or a more relaxed look with things gathered on worktops or hanging from hooks?
- Where will you locate extra items like the hi-fi, computer if you have one, and so on?

LIVING ROOMS

FAR LEFT: In a spacious house with many rooms, or a city pied-à-terre with one or two occupants, the living room needn't be stuffed with clutter. Celebrate that by building generous open-shelf display space: you can always 'grow into' the shelves as possessions build up.

LEFT: In a family room used for playing and relaxing, it's a good idea to devote a wall to cupboards. Toys can come out by day, and be hidden away for grown-up ambience at night.

ASSESSING USE OF THE ROOM

These days the living room must be all things to all people. As well as socializing in it, we expect to watch TV, listen to music, read and use the computer. In a family home, children may wish to practise musical instruments or play games. Often, the formal sitting room has been swallowed up entirely, and the 'living room' is a seating area off a large kitchen/dining room. The secret to attaining a calm, ordered space is to crystallize how you want to use it, and plan storage to keep clutter at bay.

Once you've listed key activities, think through the accompanying equipment that needs to be stored. As well as obvious large items such as a TV or piano, there might be sheet music, books, sewing kit, DVDs and more. Add to that list any collections held in this room, from photo albums to reference books. Use the checklists at the end of the chapter to build a personalized record. This is also the time to ask yourself whether everything *currently* stored in the sitting room deserves to remain there. If space is tight, could board games be rehoused in a playroom, paperwork moved to a tiny home office?

LEFT: **In a room that doubles as a sitting room and home library, it is both sensible and decorative to plan floor-to-ceiling bookshelves. The room has been cleverly zoned, with angled lamps and a leather sofa at the reading end, a fireside chair at the other. The butted-up free-standing shelves and the rakish arrangement of the books provide a relaxed format. There's a sense that, as the book collection grows, shelving can be added to on an adjacent wall.**

ABOVE: **In a room devoted to quiet contemplation and grown-up entertaining, storage is less about clutter control, and more about planning ways to show off treasured accessories. In this room, a long narrow shelf provides ample space for paintings or photographs. It would look equally good stacked with a neat line of hardbacks or piles of magazines.**

Whether the living room is a relaxed open-plan space, a family snug or a formal sitting room will also affect the storage you choose. In a busy home, casual open shelves and easy-access low cupboards make sense. A grown-up entertaining space, on the other hand, may require clutter to be banned, with the emphasis on decorative accessories. Remember that a living room gives a big clue to our personalities. Visitors love nothing better than checking out your book or music collection. Hide away too much, and you will rob the living room of its true character.

IDENTIFYING A STYLE

Shelves and cupboards can take up a substantial amount of wall space, so it's vital that storage looks good. Too often, we start to plan long after key decisions are made on furniture or colour, resulting in conflicting styles. Reverse that trend. If you are doing building work, and want to blend great storage into the fabric of the building, then choose it early, alongside hard finishes. If you're organized enough to prepare a mood board for each room, remember to include pictures of potential storage styles alongside the fabric swatches and paint cards.

Always look to your home's architecture for inspiration. Prominent features, such as glazed internal doors or Thirties Crittall windows, may provide

ABOVE LEFT: **Beautifully designed storage can have as much impact as a great sofa, so try to think of shelves as pieces of furniture, rather than just storage solutions. These wall-mounted open units, in a mix of sizes and door fronts, look abstract and funky in a contemporary sitting room.**

ABOVE RIGHT: **It may be an obvious solution to fit fireplace alcoves with floor-to-ceiling shelves, but they can look uninspired. In this classical sitting room, the design gains interest from a grid of shelf dividers, nicely echoing the glazed internal door. Central, narrow shelves have been tailored to keep CDs in order.**

LEFT, ABOVE AND BELOW: **Not everyone wants possessions on display, finding that rows of books or boxes can jar with a tranquil scheme. 'Secret' cupboards, built into natural alcoves, then concealed with a wall of MDF panelling, are a clever alternative. In a small room, this device gives the illusion of extra space.**

a starting point for storage designs throughout, and means the new storage will blend sympathetically. A loft space, by contrast, may inspire scaled-up cupboards to match large proportions, or the use of industrial materials. In the absence of good features, your existing furniture may prompt a design direction. If you already own contemporary sofas and a wenge sideboard, then built-in cupboards with matching wenge doors are an option.

As well as using design books and magazines for solutions, allocate a few days to trawling the shops. Even if you're planning bespoke storage, designer pieces may inspire with their shape, finish or size. Likewise, elements of high-street designs may be incorporated into the concept. Examine free-standing pieces in tandem, from modern to antique, as the most interesting-looking rooms combine both. If you are planning fitted cupboards in solid wood, ask a local timber supplier or your joiner to show you unusual examples to spark off ideas.

THIS PAGE: **The advantage of early planning, while building work is still in progress, is that you can design multi-purpose storage that doubles as furniture. This low, modern bench runs the length of the room, yet has useful niches for storage baskets and logs.**

ABOVE, LEFT AND RIGHT: **In a large room or loft space, built-in shelves and cupboards can act as a room divider. This one has bookshelves on the sitting-room side, and a TV on the reverse in the bedroom. At each end, flush cupboards conceal the wiring. In a period knocked-through living room, free-standing furniture may be more appropriate. A console, with shelves below, will divide the space without ruining proportions.**

RIGHT: **Allow for flexibility when planning niche shelving. Here, the lowest shelf provides extra room for ad hoc lighting or decorative accessories.**

FAR RIGHT: **Check proportions before investing in a large free-standing piece, so that it doesn't overpower the room. Painted wood or mirrored furniture looks especially unobtrusive.**

OPPOSITE: **The retro sideboard has become a modern-day classic in the sitting room. It combines good internal capacity – perfect for hiding the stereo and DVD player – yet provides plenty of display space on top.**

BUILT-IN VERSUS FREE-STANDING

Plan built-in furniture with its decorative impact in mind. Flush cupboards look efficient in the kitchen, but living-room storage needs a little more soul. Door fronts should be elegant, shelf trims nicely detailed. Built-in storage is meant to conceal clutter, but you don't want the sitting room to resemble an office.

Built-in storage includes bookshelves, cupboards, wall-mounted units, niche shelving or banks of drawers. Consider the potential for adding joinery. Look at natural alcoves flanking a chimneybreast, or a disused fireplace cavity. In a tall room, shallow cupboards close to the ceiling look dramatic; in a tiny room, a wall-mounted bench shelf is streamlined and hides storage beneath. Try out storage in less usual places, such as shelves around a door frame, or running above an aperture between two rooms.

The advantages of built-in are that you get personalized storage, can use every spare centimetre, and it adds a sophisticated finish. It's not cheap, but always an excellent investment. Find a good joiner who can interpret your sketches or ideas. And be specific. You'll need measurements – everything from book heights to the size of the TV – as well as requirements for shelf trims and thickness, whether cupboards should be flush or proud, and the finish or materials for doors. Sometimes (not always) it can be cost-effective to customize shop-bought units.

Choosing free-standing furniture is less of a leap of faith. You can pick pieces not just for capacity, but because they are beautiful. Antique buys will also lend a unique character to the room. The most obvious choices include bookcases, sideboards, armoires or burcaux. But think, too, of side tables, elegant drawer units and ottomans or trunks.

BOOKSHELVES

Bookshelves add individuality to the living room. Whether filled with books, CDs or photo albums, they provide a constant reminder of our favourite things, as well as the suggestion that – at any time – we might sit down with something good to read. For the visitor, well-filled bookshelves are a clue to the owner's personality, and generate an intimate, all-enveloping mood. Shelves needn't be filled with books: used as a display area, they can just as easily hold art or special photos.

So, unless you are after a truly minimalist space, totally devoid of clutter, it's vital to plan for good-

quality shelves. Shoddy versions will buckle easily with the weight of books, and cheapen a well-furnished room. Conversely, quality, bespoke bookshelves always provide a good-looking decorative backbone. Plan them properly so they will 'grow' with your collection. For the committed paperback lover, it can look smart to purpose-build shelves to fit their exact dimensions, adding empty shelves for growth. Alternatively, choose shelves with an adjustable racking system, so the height can adapt to changing book sizes over time.

Decide early on whether you want bookshelves to blend into the room or make a decorative statement. MDF shelves painted the colour of the walls will

ABOVE AND RIGHT: **Built-in shelves can look as beautiful as a free-standing bookshelf. This unit, with its elaborately fluted detailing and dark veneer, looks as good with modern furniture as it would teamed with antique pieces. Large-scale, wall-mounted shelving must, however, have proper wall support, so check with the joiner or builder what is required. Scale is crucial, too. Ensure that the shelves have sufficient 'breathing space' at top and bottom, so as not to overpower the room.**

look discreet, and will automatically throw attention onto the books or accessories on display. If you favour statement shelves, they may be in a dominant wood veneer, painted a contrast colour, or constructed in glass or steel. Under-shelf lighting looks particularly dramatic. How you arrange items is as crucial as what you put onto the shelves. Too few accessories can look just as distracting as an overflowing surplus of books. Play around to get the best arrangement. Experiment with a mix of stacked and upright books, or prop up paintings or photographs between the spines.

DEALING WITH ENTERTAINMENT

We live in a media-saturated world. Most of us have a TV, not to mention hi-fi, DVD player and set-top box to store, plus the accompanying collections of DVDs and CDs. These days, technology is so stylish that fewer people worry about concealing it. There are wall-mounted plasma or LCD TVs, or flat-screen versions, and most associated kit is good-looking.

Yet for those who want a sleek, grown-up living room, it's still crucial to cover up media. If you don't mind the TV screen, but just don't want it taking pride of place, niche storage is ideal. Either utilize an existing cavity (such as where a fireplace has been removed), or create one by building the TV into a new plasterboard wall. Ensure there's adequate ventilation. If built-in storage is impossible, consider a flexible TV arm, so the television is tucked into a corner when not in use, or nestle the television onto a built-in shelf, among books and accessories.

If you want everything hidden, a built-in cupboard is the best alternative. Everything can be concealed behind single or double, sliding, shuttered or flap-down doors. Think about logistics. The television should sit low, for easy viewing, whereas the DVD, hi-fi and so on can be higher. If doors stand open for viewing, will they impede human traffic flow?

If you prefer free-standing furniture, customize the inside of a Chinese cabinet, retro sideboard or armoire to hold the essentials, boring holes for the cables at the back. Alternatively, the high street has good-looking TV cabinets, often with drawers underneath or shelves for the set-top box and DVD player. And don't forget to organize the remote controls. A leather or wicker tray, to match your style of furnishings, will keep everything neatly together.

RIGHT: **Play with scale when you are planning niche storage. The size and sophistication of this grey-painted unit turn the TV into an eye-catching feature, rather than simply concealing it. DVDs and videos are stored in boxes on top.**

THIS PAGE: **Properly planned in advance, TV storage can be sorted at the same time as planning all-purpose living-room cupboards. In this sitting room, the television is usefully located in the bottom cupboard.**

OPPOSITE: **This beautifully designed wall unit seamlessly conceals all technology, yet in a quirky, casual way. While the lower niches, with flap-down doors, hold stereo and radio, the higher cupboards store CDs and DVDs. Flush doors, with touch-catches, mean the unit all but disappears when not in use, yet the style still complements the panelled room. It's trickier to hide stereo speakers behind doors. Installing ceiling speakers provides the most seamless finish.**

ABOVE: **In a small room, wall-mounted magazine racks, perhaps on the side of a bookshelf, are a quick-access solution. Keep them shallow so it is easy to find things. Regular sort-outs will keep storage working smoothly. Recycle newspapers, tear and file articles, and stack magazines horizontally on designated shelves.**

OPPOSITE: **There's an art to planning storage for frequently used items. They must be easy to access, so open shelves are better than cupboards, yet organized enough to look attractive. These narrow shelves, at convenient hand height, keep CDs tidy and break up a bank of doors.**

ORGANIZING CLUTTER

It's often the smaller, everyday clutter – from paperbacks to matches – that threatens to disrupt the visual peace in the living room. Plan for that, and look out for elegant boxes, baskets or racks that will suit your decorative theme. These days high-street stores have attractive versions in leather, sisal, fabric or perspex, designed to hold everything from magazines to CDs. In a rustically inspired living room, pile things casually into a selection of wicker baskets. A modern room, by contrast, might benefit from a steel magazine carrier and wall-mounted CD rack. You might even consider adding fabric pockets to loose-covered armchairs, for the daily newspaper.

Even the best of us need to conceal mess in a hurry sometimes. So plan quick-tidy solutions, too. An ottoman with a lift-up lid, lacquered trunk or large rectangular basket, tucked below a side table, are all ways to cover up. A coffee table with a shelf underneath is the ideal way to sort neatly stacked magazines, while a side table with drawers can hold private papers. Choose attractive storage for specifics such as fire logs, tea lights and sewing kit, and make sure everyone knows what's where.

Just as storage seeks to cover up most possessions, there will be favourite things you'll want on show. If you've planned built-in storage, allocate at least one shelf for display, preferably between waist height and eye level. Don't use it as a dumping ground, but consciously choose decorative articles – from family photos to an antique piece of china – which you, and your visitors, will enjoy. Concentrate on scale. A deep, high shelf needs to be well filled with generously proportioned items to look good. Use the surfaces of free-standing furniture for display, too.

BELOW: **Media hardware storage is one of the trickiest to plan, because if the systems don't work perfectly people will be less likely to replace items. Most of us also have to cope with a mix of entertainment sizes: among the CDs and DVDs will still be favourite videos and tapes. If there's the budget, purpose-built drawers are a wonderful solution. Failing that, open plastic or steel racks, lined up on shelves or inside a cupboard, are the answer. Avoid CD boxes with lids; although they stack conveniently, they are more time-consuming to access and you can't see at a glance.**

LIVING ROOM CHECKLISTS

ITEMS TO ACCOMMODATE

EQUIPMENT
Television, DVD or video player

Hi-fi and speakers

Computer

ENTERTAINMENT ITEMS
Books and reference books

DVDs and/or videos, CDs, computer
games

Photographs – boxes or albums

Magazines and newspapers

Board games and puzzles

DECORATIVE ITEMS
Paintings and wall hangings

Accessories

Table and reading lamps

USEFUL ITEMS
Candles and matches

Logs

Sewing kit

Greetings cards and wrapping paper

ISSUES TO ADDRESS

- Is this a casual, family sitting room where lots of different activities need to coincide?
- Or a formal sitting room, designed for conversation and music?
- How much extra space remains for storage, once the key pieces of furniture have been included?
- Do you prefer the look of fitted shelves and cupboards, or unfitted pieces?
- How can you adapt and/or extend existing storage?
- What is your budget – low or high?
- Should storage make a statement or blend in?

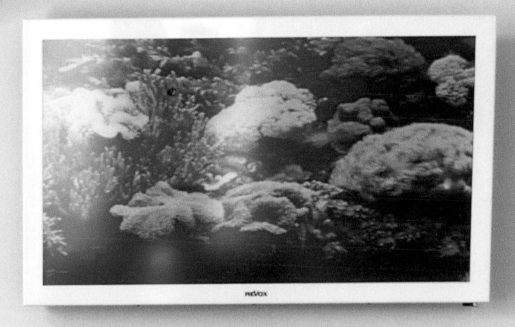

MEDIA ROOMS

THIS PAGE: **In this family media room, the owners have opted for a careful mix of hi-tech good looks and more informal storage systems. The wide-screen plasma TV takes centre stage, yet saves space because it is wall-mounted, while the DVD player et al are neatly concealed in a retro-style cabinet. Plenty of open shelves hold books, magazines and CDs. There's an extra advantage to planning streamlined storage, as it frees up floor space for comfortable furniture to lounge on.**

ASSESSING USE OF THE ROOM

The media room is increasingly common in the twenty-first century home, but it requires a whole new decorative rule book. While we continue to agonize over having technology on view in the sitting room, in a media room the equipment is the star. The way you house it must combine streamlined good looks, practicality and flexibility. Added to that, the room's proportions may be less than generous. Popular spots for a new media room include a spare bedroom or a basement conversion, which may have lower than average ceilings, so storage must be particularly hard-working.

First, compile a list of the technology you plan to include. As well as the TV, there will be a DVD and/or VCR player, set-top box and perhaps surround-sound speakers. Think of the hi-fi system, which may be micro or separates, depending on how seriously you take your music. For retro fans, there will be a record turntable. The media room is also the place to house the PS2 or Xbox, computer, extras such as a karaoke system or children's dance mat, or – for the teen technology freak – mixing desks.

Think about how many people will use the room, and the mood you want to create. In a smarter room that doubles as a second sitting room, sophisticated built-in cupboards will be the order of the day. In a casual family room, open shelves are better. Do you have small children? Equipment may need to be housed out of their reach. Human traffic flow must also come into the equation. You won't want the wall of TV and storage next to the room's only entry point, as people coming in will impede viewing. If it is important to cater for concurrent activities, the room must be zoned according to TV-viewing, computer use and a reading corner.

Consider budget. If you're after a hi-spec room, and have the finance, then get a specialist home entertainment company to plan the technology, and how to store it. But it's perfectly possible to plan great storage yourself. Research the technological options, including useful little extras such as cord controllers and all-in-one remote controls, all of which contribute to a seamless finish. And remember that flexible storage is vital. Equipment changes constantly, so shelves and cupboards will need to adapt as you add or alter technology.

RIGHT: **If planning bespoke storage for a conventional TV, remember to keep it at low level in a media room. The whole point of a dedicated room is that everything is geared towards relaxation, so expect kids to view on the floor, grown-ups lying on the sofa. Measure your existing furniture and work out a user-friendly viewing height. The top of a long, lean cabinet doubles as display space. The media room is the ideal spot to show off family photos or treasured possessions.**

MEDIA STORAGE

The focal point will always be the television. How you house it will affect all other storage plans, so make this decision early on. Fitted solutions include creating a purpose-built niche, adding a deep alcove within a wall of shelving, or siting it within a built-in low cabinet. Allow adequate ventilation to avoid overheating. In a small room, you'll save space by choosing a wall-mounted plasma or LCD screen, though it's not cheap; alternatively, sit a conventional TV on a retractable wall bracket. Remember that the set-top box and DVD player needn't be stored next to the TV, but if space is really tight you can choose a model with built-in DVD and VCR players.

A more relaxed look is achieved by housing the TV in a free-standing cabinet. In a smart room, opt for a purpose-built piece, with beautifully veneered doors or sliding shutters. A modern media space, by contrast, looks good with a purpose-built TV stand in steel and glass. Many feature shelves below to house accompanying kit. Other versions might include a TV trolley on castors, an entertainment 'bench' that holds the TV on top and DVD drawers below, or a full-height, open-plan unit.

Storing the hi-fi is equally important. Match the storage to the style you possess. A slim CD player, for example, can be wall-mounted to show off a good design, whereas a complex bank of CD and cassette players, plus amplifiers, is better off behind a door. A micro hi-fi system can be neatly housed on a built-in shelf. Where will the speakers go? In a chic media room, mount them on a specialist stand, but in a family room, it's safer to tuck speakers onto a shelf or to wall-mount them. Many come in attractive wood veneers or brushed aluminium.

THIS PAGE: **When planning a unit to hold all media systems, measure up carefully and talk to your joiner. As well as looking good, the unit must allow sufficient ventilation for all technology. Don't forget to add enough space above a CD player with a slide-up door, and add holes at the back for cables to feed through.**

OPPOSITE: **This is a particularly sophisticated take on how to conceal the TV. When not in use, the screen is covered up with beautifully crafted walnut sliding doors to match the wall-mounted unit below. The doors 'disappear' into the wall when pushed back.**

THIS PAGE: **No one wants to be reminded of household paperwork while chilling out in a media room. Keep the computer and everyday filing systems out of view in an alcove, preferably hidden behind a conventional or sliding door. Allow room under the worktop to slide in a stool when not in use.**

OPPOSITE: **It's helpful to segregate concealed technology in one cupboard, with everyday storage in another. This barrage of hi-fi equipment disappears behind a chic timber door.**

SMALL STORAGE SOLUTIONS

Precisely because the media room is designed for relaxing, it must be expertly planned to keep clutter from view. Once the technology is sorted, think through the minutiae. How will you accommodate all the CDs, DVDs, videos and cassettes? There are myriad high-street options, including wall-mounted steel towers, curved racks or cubes. Yet you'll get a neater finish with open-topped boxes or racks, lined on a shelf or within a cupboard. Purpose-built drawers, or a shop-bought media unit with drawers, will keep them in order. Don't overspend on this type of storage, as music is increasingly downloaded from, and stored on, the computer.

Plan built-in or open-shelf storage to house some bigger boxes or baskets, which can take extras such as headphones or a computer-game joystick, none of which looks especially beautiful out on display. Depending on how family-friendly you wish the media room to be, quick-access storage might also be needed for PS2 or Xbox equipment. A deep drawer or shelf might also be allocated to the digital camera and/or camcorder, plus accompanying cables, or a portable DVD player.

If you don't have a separate home office, and the media room must also double as a computer zone, consider where to house the terminal, hard drive and printer. If you want a slick-looking room, with only bespoke storage and the TV on view, then consider making cupboards extra deep so that a pull-out computer desk, with shelves above, can be concealed. In a relaxed chill-out den, a zinc-topped table or glass trestle, with a storage unit on castors pushed underneath, is ideal. Add a stool with a lift-up lid for storing paper, and the finish will be seamless.

MEDIA ROOM CHECKLISTS

ITEMS TO ACCOMMODATE

EQUIPMENT
Television
DVD or video player, set-top box
Computer and printer
Radio

SPECIALIST EXTRAS
Digital camera, video camera
Headphones
Karaoke system
Computer-games console and/or joystick

SMALL ITEMS
CDs
DVDs or videos
Computer games
Pens, art materials, paints, etc.
Games and jigsaw puzzles
Magazines and books

- Is there the potential to include built-in storage, particularly important if the room is small?
- Do you prefer media equipment to be on show or seamlessly shut away when not in use?
- Is it preferable to have drawers, closed cupboards or open shelves for smaller items?
- How many people will be using the room, and how many activities does it need to cater for?
- Is the room to be shared by grown-ups and children, or do you want a sophisticated media space?

STUDIES AND OFFICES

THIS PAGE: **It's still possible to use office-style storage, even if a study zone is tucked into another room. The secret is clever accessorizing: a curvy lamp and comfortable swivel chair tie in the desk area with the cosy sitting room.**

ASSESSING USE OF THE ROOM

In the age of the computer and flexible working, many of us now have a home office. Those who work from home need a formalized space. Others are in search of a quiet, relaxed study for paperwork. If you're not sure whether you need a home office, give it serious thought. However tiny, a well-organized study can become the nerve centre of the whole house. We all have documents and possessions that we must keep, yet which inevitably clutter our principal living spaces. Plan good storage space for them here, and let the rest of your home 'breathe'.

If possible, allocate a whole room, such as a loft conversion or boxroom, for the study. Alternatively, designate a specific corner of a sitting room or kitchen, or double up: a spare bedroom or dining room can usefully be combined with a home office. Space-planning will be crucial, as most offices are small, yet must include certain specific kit. If there is

ABOVE: **In a living room that must include a study area, plan customized bookshelves with an integral desk for a seamless finish. The worktop may be continuous with other shelves, or designed as a flap-down section. Small units with doors will conceal office paraphernalia, while a few discreet cubby holes can hold stationery or even the printer.**

LEFT: **The most discreet ad hoc home office combines a cleared, decent-sized table to hold the laptop, with more permanent wall-mounted storage for reference books. A large sideboard in the sitting room has drawers for household paperwork, as well as room for the entertainment system.**

no available room, can you squeeze a work area into an under-stairs cavity or convert space on a landing?

Who will use the office, for what activities, and at which times of the day, will directly affect planning. For home-based workers, who may even need to hold meetings here, a smart, perfectly organized space with lots of built-in cupboards is vital. In a family home, where you do paperwork by day and the kids use the computer in the evening, a large desk and individualized storage will help. Two adults, by contrast, may require twin work zones, but can share cupboard space. If the 'office' is integrated within one of the principal rooms, then a floor-to-ceiling cupboard, with retractable computer shelf, will conceal the work area at night.

PLANNING SHELVES AND CUPBOARDS

Capacious shelves and/or cupboards are the lifeblood of a good office. Acquaint yourself with what must be stored, using the checklists at the end of the chapter. There may also be job-related items that demand customized storage. Architects will need plan drawers, an artist vertical pigeonholes for frames, while a knitter needs shallow shelves for wool. Return to your storage personality. Do you want closed doors, or easy-access shelf storage?

Customized storage is often the best solution for a small room. Consider floor-to-ceiling shelving on one wall, plus an L-shaped desk to maximize corner space. Or arrange everything on one wall, with shelves above, a built-in worktop, and filing cabinets tucked below. Where there are tall ceilings, add top cupboards for infrequently used items, or line every wall in a study with bookshelves. Fitted cupboards with sliding or roll-up fabric panel doors take up less space than conventional hinged doors. Match the style of storage to the required mood. Industrial materials like steel, laminate or plywood look modern and suit a formal environment; wood veneers or funky coloured plastics are more relaxed.

Also check out off-the-peg options. There's a huge choice of storage, from inexpensive to designer. Steer clear of the real budget offerings, as some are badly made and will buckle easily. Before going shopping measure key equipment, from the printer to box files, to ensure everything will fit, and remember that domestic shelving can be less expensive compared to designated office storage. There's a lot of fun in customizing ordinary shelves. Avoid buying a matching range, and instead mix open shelves with cube units, or paint shelves for an individual finish.

ABOVE: **If the office zone is part of a larger room, it's vital to keep open shelves looking good. Colour-coded boxes are very effective. Storage containers come in a vast array of designs, from fabric- or wallpaper-covered to leather, metal or plywood, so pick a style to suit the decor.**

LEFT: **When devising open shelves, work out how you will organize them. If there's lots of paperwork, box files will do the trick, or use an assortment of stacking cardboard boxes, open-topped baskets or see-through acrylic containers to contain clutter.**

OPPOSITE: **If shelves are cleverly planned, it's even possible to fit an 'office' into a tiny space behind a door. This open arrangement, in utility materials, combines in little everything the typical office needs. The unit is deep enough to hold the computer, with a pull-out keyboard shelf, but there's also a bookshelf, and individual little drawers to keep small objects in order. The sand-blasted glass partition prevents the office zone from encroaching on more formal living space.**

OPPOSITE: **An integrated desk and storage unit, in jolly colours, makes for a user-friendly, yet good-looking study. Check out modern furniture stores, as many stock modular ranges designed for any room in the house, which can be cleverly adapted for home studies.**

RIGHT: **For a more formal office, a matching set of open cube storage, cabinets on castors and a double desk arrangement creates a chic, efficient mood. The long worktop allows enough space for extras such as a CD player.**

CHOOSING OFFICE FURNITURE

The style of the desk can make or break a home office. It must be deep enough to accommodate the computer and keyboard, plus essentials such as a lamp and telephone. Look for styles that incorporate a couple of slim drawers, or a traditional pedestal, with twin columns of drawers. Many desks, however, aren't capacious enough. Instead, adapt a trestle table or small dining table, or find a high-street store that supplies lengths of glass, MDF or steel worktop, with a choice of self-assembly leg styles. Storage cabinets can be usefully slotted underneath.

Every office needs a filing cabinet. Those with deep suspension drawers provide easy access to paperwork, whereas styles with shallow drawers are brilliant for stationery. Pick one with a selection of drawer widths if there's just space for a single cabinet. As well as office-supply stores, check out home shops, as many have attractive home-office ranges. Second-hand office suppliers or junk shops are more unusual sources. It really matters that the filing cabinet functions well; unless drawers open smoothly, no one will be motivated to do the filing.

Adding more free-standing furniture will be dictated by your storage needs and available room. You don't have to use office furniture. In a formal setting, a sideboard, drawer unit or chic wooden cabinet can hold stationery supplies, while the top accommodates the printer and fax. Also look out for smart modular storage units, combining open-shelf and cupboard variations, to give a sleek, designer finish. A relaxed study might include a glass-fronted cabinet, a metal school locker or an armoire, all of which look decorative and can be customized internally with shelves and containers.

ORGANIZING PAPERWORK

We may wish that the paperless office had arrived, but in reality most households battle with copious amounts of paperwork. As well as essential bills and documents, there may be school notices, social correspondence, bank statements and magazine cuttings to be stored, not to mention newspapers, catalogues and holiday brochures. If you work from home, the amount of paperwork can triple. Rule number one, of course, is to have regular sort-outs. The home filing system should contain only this year's documents, and out-of-date publications (favourite magazines excepted) must be thrown away. And certain documents are just as easily stored on computer disk, without being printed.

Before deciding on the best storage system for you, it's worth mentally dividing paperwork into current, such as bills to be paid and stuff to be filed;

this year's, such as holiday plans or school info; and permanent, including documents such as passports and birth certificates. These categories will help you decide which files stay desk-top, which go on shelves and which can go in a cupboard. Some people forget current paperwork if it's in a file. In this case, pile it into open trays or display it on a giant metal pinboard. This month's magazines and catalogues can be stacked into a wicker basket.

As well as the all-purpose filing cabinet, good-quality cardboard files will keep paperwork sorted on shelves. Sturdy magazine holders keep periodicals neat, lever-arch files are good for massed paperwork, and box files excellent for organizing different-sized leaflets. Letters and postcards you want to keep can be piled into flat A4 cardboard boxes, while 'memento' paperwork is best stuck in a scrapbook. Enjoy choosing your files and boxes. There are many attractive ranges to buy, or customize your own.

OPPOSITE: **It's a good idea to combine several types of paperwork storage. As well as traditional shelf files, consider small tabletop drawer units, which can be used to keep current correspondence sorted. A traditional office spike, paperweights marked 'Now' or 'Tomorrow', or a series of labelled filing trays are also good alternatives to keep 'live' paperwork in order. Include a letter rack or post tray to keep incoming mail organized. Wall-mounted bulldog clips, above the desk, are good ways to display newspaper cuttings, such as new recipes to try or a shop to visit.**

THIS PAGE: **For any filing system to work effectively, it must be carefully labelled. You might wish to colour-code different categories, or file by date or alphabetical order. Keep labelling specific, so that it's always easy to find a particular document.**

DESK SOLUTIONS

In an ideal world, we'd all have an empty desktop, save the computer, a telephone and work-in-progress. Too often, we battle with a cluttered desk. The answer is to utilize the space that's within easy reach once sitting down. If there is a wall in front of the desk, fix a few shelves at seated head height, to hold frequently used files or paper trays. If you're planning a purpose-built unit, deepen the desktop to include raised pigeonholes at the back.

Don't fill up the desktop with computer-related technology. Locate the printer, fax and shredder on a nearby table or cabinet. If there's a separate hard drive, store it on a purpose-designed trolley on wheels, tucked under the desk, or slot it onto a low shelf, ensuring there is adequate ventilation. A great option, frequently used in commercial offices, is an L-shaped arrangement. On one surface keep the

computer and telephone, and on the other, at right angles, arrange filing trays or current periodicals. A swivel chair moves you easily from one to the other.

As for the inevitable bits and bobs, from a calculator to pencils, choose attractive yet user-friendly containers. Find designs that are more imaginative than the classic desk-tidy options. Pens can be organized into a shallow desk drawer, or stashed in a glass cube vase or pottery beaker. Tiny essentials, such as paper clips and drawing pins, can be sorted into an acrylic multi-drawer container or pooled into small open bowls. Add hooks to a nearby shelf and hang up scissors, sellotape and the hole punch. And have a strict house rule. If anyone borrows 'office' essentials, they must always remember to put them back.

ABOVE: **Not everything in the office fits into neat drawers and shelves. Bulky items, including Jiffy bags and bubble wrap, can be piled into a large basket, tucked below the desk.**

LEFT: **If desk space is really cramped, switching from a bulky computer terminal to a laptop can make an appreciable difference. As an alternative to an L-shape, consider a square desk configuration. Here, the work zone with computer, printer and lamp is on one side, with the far side used for extra worktop storage.**

RIGHT: **Double available space by adding tiered built-in shelves above the worktop – also a useful trick to provide privacy. Multi-layered trays and pigeonholes increase space, too.**

STUDY AND OFFICE CHECKLISTS

ITEMS TO ACCOMMODATE

EQUIPMENT
Computer
Printer
Fax machine
Shredder
Radio/television

DESK KIT
Filing trays
Pen holders
Stationery/stamps
Computer disks
Scissors, sellotape, hole punch, etc.

ESSENTIAL ITEMS
Box, lever-arch and concertina files
Reference books
Correspondence and paperwork
Magazines/periodicals
Jiffy bags/bubble wrap
Lamp
Telephone

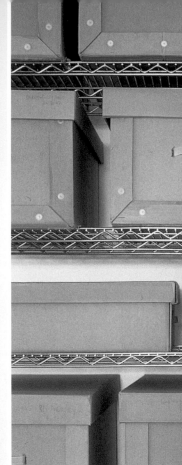

ISSUES TO ADDRESS

- How large/small is the available room? Is it for one person, or to be shared?
- How organized are you (honestly), and how likely are you to tidy up daily?
- Do you prefer everything tidied behind cupboard doors, or on easy-access open-shelf storage?
- Do you want a neat, workmanlike mood or a cosy, relaxed study?
- Is there the budget for built-in shelves and cupboards, or can you customize high-street furniture?
- Do you prefer work in progress to be neatly filed, or out on display?

UTILITY ROOMS

THIS PAGE: **If space is very tight, an efficient utility zone can still be arranged along one wall of a small room. This laundry zone makes maximum use of a tiny space, with the washing machine and dryer stacked one on top of the other, deep pull-out shelves for towels and sheets, and room on the floor for laundry baskets.**

OPPOSITE: **If there's no space for an ironing board proper, a sturdy retractable shelf for pressing clothes can be custom-built.**

ASSESSING USE OF THE ROOM

A utility room will work wonders for the smooth running of the household. If everyone knows where to dump dirty laundry and find clean clothes, there will be less mess in the bathroom or on the kitchen floor. The basic essentials to be housed will include the washing machine and dryer (or washer-dryer if space is tight), laundry baskets, washing powders and the ironing board and iron. It's also the ideal place to store household essentials such as shoe polishing stuff, spare light bulbs, vases and so on. If space permits, outdoor coats, sports kit and cleaning equipment will also find a home here.

You don't need a large room, but efficient space-planning is vital so that there's both room to complete domestic tasks and enough storage space. If you don't have a utility room, consider where one might be added. A small room adjacent to the kitchen or an upstairs bathroom is ideal. Alternatively, you could convert a dry cellar or garage (with access from the house), or add a utility zone under the stairs. The amount of space you allocate should depend on the size of the household.

Use the checklist at the end of the chapter to help you compile a personalized list, not just of what must be stored, but of how you plan to use the room. Is this just a space for doing the washing, or will you iron in here too? Does your home have a separate airing cupboard for sheets and towels, or should there be racks for storing fresh laundry? Will laundry be sorted here – in which case you'll need sufficient worktop space – and will there be hand washing, requiring a small sink? Finally, do you have access to outdoors, or must clothes be dried and aired in the utility room?

THIS PAGE: **Space can be 'stolen' from a wide passageway to create a utility zone concealed behind built-in, flush-fronted cupboards.**

OPPOSITE: **Specialist storage solution retailers, plus some high-street stores, make good hunting grounds for clever extras such as pull-out ironing boards, drying racks and drawer or shelf organizers.**

PLANNING SHELVES AND CUPBOARDS

Fitted cupboards with flush doors that conceal everything including the washing machine and dryer are ideal if you want mess to be contained. This is important if the utility zone is incorporated under the stairs or is part of another room, such as a downstairs loo. Behind the doors, plan a comprehensive selection of shelves, remembering to include enough worktop to accommodate at least two ironing baskets (one for dirty, one for clean), as well as a niche for the laundry bin. Good design choices for flush doors include painted MDF, tongue-and-groove panelling, laminate or plywood.

In a utility room in daily use, it's more sensible to stick to open-plan shelves, leaving the washing machine and dryer fronts on display. Site the shelves immediately above the machines, so washing powders are within reach. You might combine the shelves with high built-in cupboards for bulk-buy household supplies and, if there's room, a full-height cupboard for the Dyson, mops and broom. Add a row of sturdy hooks, for hanging up everything from the peg basket to a dustpan and brush. Have fun choosing shelf materials. As well as painted MDF, you might play up the working theme with zinc, steel mesh or slatted wood shelves.

For those wanting a less streamlined finish, check out high-street stores for attractive free-standing pieces. Doing the laundry has become such a hot topic that there's a great selection. A tall steel shelf unit, zinc cabinet, wood and calico unit or tiered trolley on wheels all provide great storage. Specialist pieces include a laundry trolley on wheels, with built-in laundry baskets, or an open-plan garment rail, great for storing the week's ironed shirts.

OPPOSITE: **In a utility zone on full view, such as this under-stairs arrangement, pay as much attention to appearance as to practicality. Here, good-looking wicker laundry baskets and a concealed laundry bin contribute to a seamless finish. When the lid is down, the low surface provides an ideal spot for folding freshly ironed sheets and towels.**

RIGHT: **Plan the linen cupboard with enough shelves, so that piles of sheets don't get uncomfortably high, and it's easy to organize double and single sizes plus pillowcases, table linen and so on. Either hand-write categories on the shelves, or invest in specialist linen-cupboard labels to screw onto the front of each one.**

SMALL STORAGE SOLUTIONS

Within shelves and cupboards, organize the small stuff into categories. Laundry essentials, for example, should be kept separate from dirty-job kit, such as the shoe-cleaning box. Give priority of space and accessibility to ironing. The iron should stay put on the worktop. The ironing board may be slotted into a built-in niche, or hung on the inside of a cupboard door – for really small spaces, consider a wall-hung, foldaway board. If there's no room for a concertina clothes airer, think about a ceiling-hung traditional version or a wall-mounted pull-out airer. Less-used steamers and the like can be stored in a cupboard.

Depending on the style of the room, organize smaller things into lidded plastic or metal containers, which may be stacked on a shelf. Or choose accessories designed to be shown off: a retro fabric peg bag or pretty enamel 'housekeeper's box'. Use as many specialist cupboard organizers as you can. Pull-out or wall-mounted shoe racks, shallow drawer tidies and wire shelves, designed to attach to the inside of a cupboard door, all promote order. Certain items, such as the first-aid kit and a small fire extinguisher, should be wall-mounted, in full view.

If there is enough space in the utility room for extras such as coats or sports kit, decide between built-in or more relaxed solutions. Wellies and walking boots can be neatly arranged on open-plan plywood racks or casually tossed into small metal dustbins. Coats can be hung on a pull-out rack within a cupboard, or suspended from sturdy hooks (allow sufficient space between each one for bulky jackets). And occasional kit, such as golf clubs, may be concealed in a low-level storage unit with a lift-up lid, or arranged onto a wall-mounted rack.

UTILITY ROOM CHECKLISTS

ITEMS TO ACCOMMODATE

LARGE EQUIPMENT
Washing machine

Tumble dryer

Ironing board

Vacuum cleaner

Mop and/or broom

SMALL EQUIPMENT
Laundry baskets, pegs

Indoor clothes-drying rack

Iron

Vases

Buckets, dustpan and brush

Cleaning equipment

Household supplies

Tools, shoe-cleaning kit

OTHER ITEMS
Sports kit

Coats

Wellies and boots

Clean laundry

ISSUES TO ADDRESS

- If space is at a premium, can you think laterally? What can be suspended from the ceiling or hung from hooks? Do you need room to iron and air clothes?
- Can the washing machine and tumble dryer be vertically mounted, to make space for more cupboards?
- If garden shed space is limited, does the utility room need to double up as garden tool and equipment storage space?
- Are you after a built-in or free-standing look?
- What is the budget — can high-street storage be customized rather than spending on purpose-built storage?

BEDROOMS AND DRESSING ROOMS

ASSESSING THE SPACE

Early thoughts in a bedroom should always turn to great storage. This is the one room where we expect to feel tranquil, and no one can relax with clothes strewn about. There's an increasing trend to shift storage out of the bedroom altogether, using a dressing room (housed in an adjacent bedroom), walk-in wardrobe or even cupboards in an en suite bathroom. But we don't all have space to spare. The key to a tranquil, organized bedroom lies in good-looking storage boasting a hard-working interior.

First, go back to basics. Draw a to-scale floor plan, including paper cut-outs of the furniture. If you're updating an existing bedroom, return to your storage inventory and check which systems work and which don't. Do you need extra capacity, better organization, or are you longing for seamless built-in cupboards? Sell or relocate free-standing furniture

RIGHT: **It's possible to achieve the convenience of built-in storage with the relaxed look of solid furniture. Inspired by the Arts and Crafts-style bed, but with a more modern mix of open and closed storage, this large wardrobe provides the ideal balance.**

OPPOSITE: **Take visual cues from the room's existing architecture. Here, built-in cupboard doors have been designed to match the existing wall panelling. In a period room, it's best to mix in some traditional pieces, such as an attractive chest of drawers or a diminutive dressing table.**

BELOW, LEFT AND RIGHT: **In this one-level apartment with tall ceilings, fitted cupboards have been added either side of the bed, as well as across the top, to maximize available space.**

that no longer works for you. If building work is possible, look at alcoves, which might hold fitted storage, consider devoting a whole wall to cupboards or plan built-in units on the bedhead wall, so that once in bed you get to view peaceful, plain walls.

Crystallize your decorative vision for the bedroom now, so that the look can be dovetailed with storage needs. In a modern room, beautifully finished fitted cupboards in dark wood veneer, sand-blasted glass or white lacquer will be appropriate. For a rustic, relaxed finish, a mix of a painted wood armoire and chests of drawers looks good; a grown-up boudoir, by contrast, might boast mirrored furniture. Add your lifestyle into the equation. Is dressing a morning rush or a leisurely affair? If a couple shares, is there room for both to access clothes at the same time?

THIS PICTURE: **With its sloping ceiling, this tiny room would have felt cramped if filled with fitted cupboards. Instead, daily clothes storage is all contained within a pretty wardrobe, while non-essentials are concealed in specialist, lidded crates pushed beneath the bed.**

THE WELL-ARRANGED INTERIOR

It's impossible to plan hard-working storage unless you take time – now – to work out what must be housed, and how often you'll need to access it. Using the checklists at the end of the chapter, arm yourself with a comprehensive list of all the clothes, accessories, books, cosmetics and other essentials that you want (or need) to store in the bedroom. If your partner is less than enthusiastic, do his or her list as well, because you'll both benefit!

Once possessions are down on paper, it's easier to divide them into categories. Devote the main body of your wardrobe to current clothes, plan less accessible space for out-of-season garments and luggage, and relocate the likes of coats and sports kit to a utility room or hall. And be ruthless. Things you no longer wear or enjoy should be given away.

We all have things that we access infrequently, but which still need a home. For bulky items such as bags or extra bedding, a capacious top cupboard, end-of-bed trunk or plastic crates on castors are all ideal. If you have a separate wardrobe in a spare bedroom, then use this to store out-of-season clothes, protected in hanging garment bags or zip-up plastic clothes bags. Alternatively, invest in a bed with built-in drawers or buy purpose-made under-bed storage boxes, bags or drawers on wheels to slot underneath.

However well-organized your main clothes storage system, plan quick-tidy solutions too. A few sturdy hooks, on the back of a door or on a wall, will encourage you to hang up clothes, or add a smart valet stand to hold clothes ready for the next day. An open wicker basket, tucked behind an armchair, is a good repository for last night's shoes.

TOP: **Floor-to-ceiling wardrobes should always incorporate a deep top shelf to accommodate things like suitcases and hatboxes. It's not essential to have separate top-cupboard doors; flush doors provide a seamless finish.**

ABOVE: **This dressing area, which links a walk-in wardrobe with the bathroom, has hooks for clothes in transit, as well as nightclothes.**

VARYING CLOTHES STORAGE OPTIONS

Every bedroom needs some hanging space, as even the jeans-and-T-shirt brigade have one smart outfit to store. Whether within a conventional or built-in wardrobe, the space rules are the same. There must be sufficient rail to allow clothes to hang freely, and enough depth to accommodate hangers (a selection of classic wood, skirt-clip and trouser-clamp styles uses space best). In a full-height wardrobe, double up men's rails top and bottom; for women, use the space below long dresses to stack shoeboxes.

Generous shelves within a wardrobe are great for piles of sweaters and T-shirts, easy to see at a glance. If you have lots of clothes, colour-coordinate garments, or divide into 'work' and 'play' categories. But only store clothes on open shelves if you are very neat (and remember that things will get dusty easily). Customized narrow shelves or pigeonholes keep shoes in order and easy to view. Wide or deep wardrobe shelves can be organized further using open-topped wicker or plastic boxes.

Smaller items such as underwear, socks, scarves and ties get muddled easily on shelves, so drawers are the best solution. Check out storage-solution shops for useful extras such as drawer organizers or expandable sock compartments. Pick a chest of drawers that offers a selection of shallow and deep drawers, or, if planning drawers within a wardrobe, wire-basket styles to let clothes 'breathe'.

Use as many specialist solutions as you can, from see-through shoeboxes and tie hangers to hatboxes and garment bags, or customize your own. The high street offers a huge range of fabric, cardboard, seagrass and plastic containers, many stackable. Use them at the base of a wardrobe or on a high shelf.

ABOVE: **The casual finish of folded clothes on shelves works best when garments are worn regularly, and rotated, so that they don't get dusty. This arrangement looks particularly good when teamed with plain walls, allowing the colours and textures of the clothes to be the star attraction. A more practical variation is to stack shelves with identical baskets or crates, giving clothes some protection.**

RIGHT: **To achieve the seamless look of a wall of built-in storage, uninterrupted by a chest of drawers, incorporate drawer storage behind closed doors. Drawers don't have to be reserved for clothes. They can also store small electrical appliances, such as the hairdryer, or cosmetics.**

OPPOSITE, LEFT: **It can be fun to merge style borders. If you prefer drawer storage, but like the built-in look, then floor-to-ceiling drawers – sunk into an alcove – give a smart twist to more traditional solutions. Additional shelves and cupboards have been added in a theme to match.**

OPPOSITE, ABOVE RIGHT: **A well-ordered cupboard interior makes getting dressed more fun, as well as keeping tidying up easy. For the committed shoe fan, floor-to-ceiling pigeonholes are a smart choice. Other shoe alternatives include stacking the original boxes, each one marked with a Polaroid picture of its contents, or using specialist boxes with flap-down ends, so shoes can be removed without disturbing the stack.**

OPPOSITE, BELOW RIGHT: **Utilize the space below a hanging rail with a modular storage system of plastic crates on wheels, or fill the cavity with the laundry bin or spare carrier bags.**

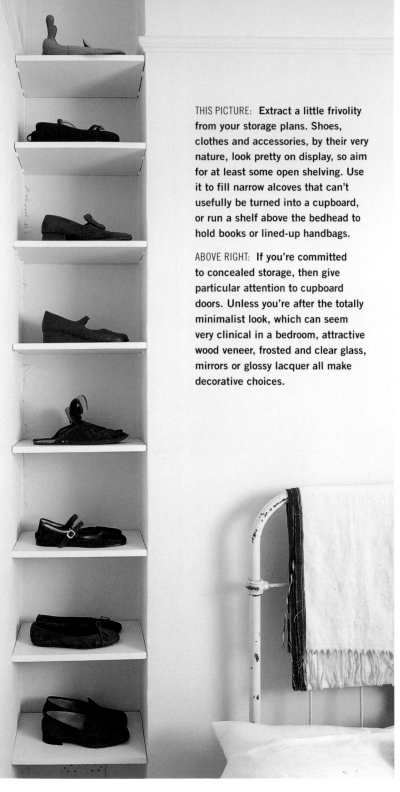

THIS PICTURE: **Extract a little frivolity from your storage plans. Shoes, clothes and accessories, by their very nature, look pretty on display, so aim for at least some open shelving. Use it to fill narrow alcoves that can't usefully be turned into a cupboard, or run a shelf above the bedhead to hold books or lined-up handbags.**

ABOVE RIGHT: **If you're committed to concealed storage, then give particular attention to cupboard doors. Unless you're after the totally minimalist look, which can seem very clinical in a bedroom, attractive wood veneer, frosted and clear glass, mirrors or glossy lacquer all make decorative choices.**

DRESSING TABLES

Perhaps as an antidote to minimalist bedrooms, the dressing table has made a welcome return. There's a good choice on the high street, from slim, modern wood-veneer styles to Thirties-inspired mirrored designs and more traditional painted versions. A good dressing table should be comfortable to sit at on a low stool, have enough depth to hold a mirror and include at least a couple of drawers. If you don't want to buy a specific piece then a pretty table, with a tiered trolley on wheels tucked underneath, will do just as well. Alternatively, build one into a bank of wall-to-wall cupboards to break up the expanse.

The dressing table's new-found popularity is all the more welcome because it provides storage for cosmetics, jewellery and accessories. If you've dispensed with a chest of drawers, this is invaluable. Take time to plan tabletop organization. In a streamlined space, arrange jewellery and make-up inside drawers; shallow drop-in drawer units or dividers can help. Or insert a grid of small containers within, categorizing possessions into earrings, necklaces, scarves and so on. See-through extras

OPPOSITE, BELOW RIGHT: **There are many wonderful drawer handles available, and they add character to banks of customized drawers. Match the style to the cupboard materials. Simple plywood or painted MDF looks good with circular cut-outs or plain metal pulls, whereas sophisticated veneers will suit neat leather tabs or elongated metal D handles. Also look out for jewel-style coloured glass knobs, aluminium handles in tactile pebble or flower shapes, and funky resin styles.**

ABOVE: **When it comes to choosing free-standing furniture such as a dressing table, don't feel compelled to select from a matching set of wardrobe, chest of drawers and bedside tables. Unless you're aiming for a streamlined finish, there's much more fun to be had from mixing and matching storage styles.**

such as plastic canisters, multiple lipstick stands and compartment make-up tidies also help.

Alternatively, turn dressing-table storage into a decorative exercise, using quirky accessories and boxes. Necklaces or rings can be hung from a jewellery tree or tiny hooks on the wall around the mirror, costume jewellery piled into open bowls, and precious things locked in a proper jewellery box. (A bedroom also needs a small safe, but stow this in a discreet location.) A dressing table is, by definition, meant to be glamorous, so enjoy making it pretty.

THIS PAGE: In a small room, it can be more useful to look at potential space behind the bed, rather than beside it. This neat built-in design incorporates shallow bookshelves, concealed behind flush doors, and a dramatically lit display shelf. Think of ways to reduce clutter. A combined clock-radio with telephone is one option.

OPPOSITE, LEFT: We all have different bedtime rituals, so match storage to your needs. If books are important, niche shelving is a smarter choice than a rakish pile on a table.

OPPOSITE, CENTRE: Measure the bed height before purchasing a cabinet or table. Essential items should be comfortably within arm's length, without the need to reach down or up.

OPPOSITE, RIGHT: A wall-mounted shelf or shelf unit is a good choice in a small room, and visually allows the floor space to 'breathe'.

BEDSIDE STORAGE

We all need to keep stuff by the bed, even if it's just a glass of water. What are your storage needs, and are they being met? After listing what you want to store, divide them into 'public' things that may go on the tabletop, and 'private', such as medicines, which are better off in a drawer. If the list is long, don't assume you need a huge bedside table. Often it's a case of pruning what you think you need: books can be stored on a shelf above the bed, make-up stowed in the bathroom, jewellery moved to a dressing table.

In a modern room, built-in bedside storage creates a lean silhouette. A shelf and/or cupboard may be incorporated into a wall-mounted bedhead, or look for a Japanese-style platform bed with a 'shelf' around the perimeter. A tiny room will benefit from a deep shelf behind the bed, rather than recesses to either side. To save space, consider wall-mounting other essentials, such as a bedside lamp, leaving more worktop for reading material and a clock.

It's tricky to find really good-looking and practical free-standing bedside tables. Although there are many useful variants, from three-drawer to closed cupboards, open shelves to a plain cube, the ideal version will feature one drawer and a deep shelf for magazines. Alternatively, opt for a plain side table, under which you can slot a large wicker basket.

CREATING A DRESSING ROOM

The vogue for creating a separate dressing room shows no sign of abating, and it's easy to understand why. As consumers, we spend increasing amounts of money on clothes and accessories, so we want to keep them neat. Plus, it feels good to keep clutter out of the bedroom. An obvious choice for a dressing room is a small adjacent bedroom, which can be linked with an interconnecting door. If the master bedroom is very large, consider building an entire wall of wardrobe storage at one end. A landing leading to the bedroom might also be converted: box it in with sliding or double doors, then line each wall with cupboards.

If you have the budget, it's worth considering a specialist storage company to plan the dressing room, kitting it out with a custom-made selection of rails, drawers, shelves and so on. But it's perfectly possible to plan your own well-organized cupboard interior. Many high-street shops offer modular wardrobe systems, which you can mix and match. Some are designed to be used free-standing (and can look good as a room divider), featuring chrome hanging rails and open-plan steel shelves. Others comprise a basic frame, which can be customized with plain or wire drawers, shelves, rails and extras such as pull-out laundry bins and shoe racks.

The advantage of a dressing room, of course, is that you can close the door on a certain amount of mess and retain a tranquil bedroom. But if you decorate and plan the dressing room as carefully as you might any other room, you'll want to keep it tidy. Add a stool for sitting on while selecting an outfit, a decent full-length mirror and good lighting, and this may well become your favourite spot in the house!

ABOVE: **If there's space, and sufficient daylight, it's a good idea to tuck in a dressing table between the banks of cupboards, so you can get dressed and made up all in one place. This neat area has been sectioned off from the main bedroom, but because the cupboards don't reach to the ceiling there's still plenty of natural light. It's also worth investing in decent lighting. Cupboards may be fitted with automatic lights, and there should be low-voltage ceiling lights on a dimmer.**

ABOVE AND OPPOSITE: **When kitting out the dressing room, buy the best-quality hanging rails and shelves that you can afford. Don't be afraid to measure your clothes, from the width of a coat on a hanger to hats, shoes and the rough dimensions of folded sweaters and T-shirts. Then plan shelves and drawers to fit. Don't forget essential extras, such as lavender bags and cedar moth protectors, to keep clothes well cared for, and an array of shoe trees to look after footwear.**

BEDROOM AND DRESSING ROOM CHECKLISTS

ITEMS TO ACCOMMODATE

CLOTHING

Full and half hanging space for dresses, shirts and suits

Folded jumpers, tops and T-shirts

Underwear and socks

Shoes/boots

Hats and hatboxes

Accessories

BULKY ITEMS

Luggage and bags

Out-of-season clothes

Sports kit

OTHER ITEMS

Spare bed linen and towels

Cosmetics

Jewellery

Magazines and books

Clock, radio, bedside light, etc.

Extra bedding and sleeping bags

ISSUES TO ADDRESS

- How minimalist and/or peaceful do you want the bedroom to be?
- What items could be rehoused in a spare bedroom or loft cupboards?
- Is there the space to create a walk-in dressing room, or at least his-and-hers closets?
- What is the budget – do you want bespoke clothes storage or to kit out the interiors with high-street internal fittings?
- Is there potential to 'steal' room from an adjacent bedroom to create more storage space?
- Do you prefer a sleek fitted look, or unfitted, with a mix of free-standing wardrobes and chests of drawers?
- How much stuff do you like to keep beside the bed?

BATHROOMS

ASSESSING SPACE AND LIFESTYLE

We may dream of having a large en suite bathroom, but a small washroom is more frequently the norm. Yet the bathroom is a hard-working room, used twice a day, every day, so it must be planned with military precision. If the existing configuration doesn't work, do consider a change of layout, fitted storage or new space-saving sanitary ware. It is an investment, but you will reap the benefits for years to come.

Whether you are starting from scratch or adding to an existing layout, arm yourself with a to-scale plan of the room, marking on fixed sanitary ware, if appropriate. Appraise the existing storage and ask yourself what is lacking. Using the checklists at the end of the chapter, prepare a list of essentials that need storing. If space is tight, can certain items go elsewhere: spare towels in the airing cupboard, or bulk-buy loo rolls in the utility room? If there's more than one bathroom, and you could do some building work, assess whether facilities might be rejigged. A tiny guest bathroom, for example, might be more user-friendly stripped of the bath and turned into a shower room with a wall of fitted cupboards.

Space-planning also depends directly on who uses the bathroom. It goes without saying that a family bathroom will need more storage, to cope with extra towels and toiletries, but it may also need to accommodate twin basins. An en suite bathroom, by its very nature, may require no more than a slim medicine cabinet, with other essentials stowed in a bedroom wardrobe. *How* the bathroom is used is also important. In a spa bathroom where you plan to linger, you'll need shelf space for reading material, whereas a wet-room shower needs little more than towel hooks and a wall-mounted soap dish.

OPPOSITE, INSET: **Planning a bathroom from scratch allows for a seamless finish. Here, cupboards for toiletries have been 'sunk' into the wall and concealed behind mirrored doors.**

OPPOSITE: **Even a no-nonsense walk-in shower needs storage for basics. This one is designed with the loo and wall-mounted shelves on a separate wall, well away from the shower jets.**

RIGHT AND BELOW: **Extra shelves are comparatively easy to add to a bathroom. If space is tight, fix them at head height. A larger room, with natural recesses, can enjoy generous shelves for towels and books.**

BUILT-IN STORAGE

If you've opted for a modern, pared-down bathroom – with fittings to match – then sleek built-in storage is essential. Few bathrooms contain architectural features, so for style inspiration cast your net wider. Take cues from your gym, a health spa or even chic hotel bathrooms. Think about steam-resistant materials for shelves or cupboards. Glass, clear or sand-blasted, laminate, stainless steel and painted MDF are all ideal. Only choose wood veneer for surfaces away from water: otherwise, hardwoods such as iroko and teak are stylish and waterproof.

In a bathroom planned from scratch, consider adding niches within a new plasterboard wall, which – if within a shower or over a bath – may be tiled to match the other walls. If planning to box in a bath or wall-mounted toilet, design the panelling to hold an extra recess for loo paper, or a space for folded towels. Plan the niche size so it looks custom-made for its contents. Not everything has to be on display. Vertical or horizontal slots, filled with seagrass baskets, can conceal less good-looking essentials such as razors or cleaning products.

A natural alcove can be fitted with a floor-to-ceiling or half-height cupboard or, in a big bathroom, an entire wall devoted to wardrobes. Blend in the style of doors with the rest of the bathroom. Sand-blasted sliding doors can be teamed with a matching shower door, say, or painted MDF panelling repeated on the bath panel. Open shelves are a good option if you can keep the contents tidy, or they may be lined with identical baskets or canisters. Shelves can fill an alcove, or fix one long, thick shelf above basins or near the bath. It will provide ample storage and look far more dramatic than several tiny ones.

ABOVE: **Even a narrow alcove can be fitted with a cupboard. In a small space, choose flush doors with touch-catches, or use minimalist handles. If a cupboard is only half-height, anticipate what will go on top. Don't let it become a dumping ground, but instead plan an attractive display.**

RIGHT: **If planning tiled niche shelving, mosaics are an ideal choice as they fit easily into a small space.**

OPPOSITE: **Built-in shelves should be shallow, so that it's easy to access what you want. They also create a natural 'frame' for whatever you put there, so keep things looking neat. Fold towels, choose pretty bottles (if necessary, decant basics into good-looking glass containers), and stow less attractive items in baskets.**

ABOVE: Provided the shelves are neat, a glass-fronted medicine cabinet will even look good full of utility items. If you don't like clutter, consider lining the glass with fabric, or replace it with translucent sand-blasted glass. Use safety glass in a family bathroom.

ABOVE RIGHT: A cabinet on wheels should have good door catches, and – if things are to be stacked on top – a rail around the perimeter to keep containers safe. A model with doors, rather than drawers, is ideal for larger items such as cleaning stuff.

FREE-STANDING STORAGE

We don't all want a fitted bathroom. There's relaxing appeal to a washroom that feels like a room, with 'furniture' including a roll-top bath, pedestal basin and floor-standing towel rail. In this case, look for pretty free-standing pieces that suit the mood. The bathroom has risen in prominence, and we expect to spend pampering time in there. In response, many stores offer cabinets, drawer units and trolleys designed for bathroom use. Proportions will be neat (tall and slim is best) and materials waterproof, including stainless steel, zinc, glass and lacquer.

Given the space restrictions, one capacious piece is probably better than two small ones. Decide whether you want to show off delicious products and folded towels, in which case a glass-fronted chemist's cabinet, vintage or new, or a small armoire fitted with chicken wire, will be ideal. For a slick look, try a metal three-drawer unit or birch veneer cabinet, while in smaller spaces a tall tiered-shelf rack or corner unit is good. Match furniture to your bathing habits. For those who want to lounge in the bath, products to hand, a tiered steel basket or old-fashioned trolley on wheels allows easy access.

If you don't want to feel boxed in by furniture, keep storage low on the floor and use casual lidded boxes or open-topped baskets. Rattan, sisal weaves and water hyacinth match most bathroom surfaces,

LEFT: A large rattan basket is the ultimate bathroom multi-tasker. It can be filled with extra loo rolls, spare towels, kids' bath toys or sponge bags. Find a useful spot to tuck it away, round the side of the bath or underneath a wall-mounted basin.

ABOVE: The best bathroom storage features shallow, narrow shelves, so that a multitude of bottles and soaps don't get in a muddle. Invest in plain glass or metal containers to organize shelves and to keep together smaller items like cotton wool or hair ties.

from stone to wood, or in a funky family bathroom consider colourful plastic crates for bath toys. You'll also need a decent laundry bin. If laundry must travel downstairs, pick a style with a removable calico liner. If space is tight, a traditional cork-topped bin that doubles as a stool is a good idea.

VANITY UNITS

Bathroom sanitary ware has altered radically in the last decade. It is more streamlined, with many wall-mounted styles, and often features elegant rounded contours. The biggest change has been in basins. The generously proportioned pedestal has given way to neater, space-saving models. Modern looks include a bowl-style basin, in ceramic, stone or wood, mounted onto a slab worktop. Basins may also be counter-sunk, with built-in cupboards beneath. The return of the vanity unit gives us more storage space, and it can double as a dressing table.

If budget (and space) is an issue, then check out high-street home stores for small-scale vanity units, complete with basin, featuring wood or laminate

THIS PAGE: **In a low-ceilinged bathroom or attic conversion with sloping roof, it makes sense to concentrate storage below worktop height and keep things looking streamlined. Solid cupboard doors conceal potential clutter, as well as all the plumbing.**

OPPOSITE, LEFT: **A generous slab of worktop, with plenty of room either side of the bowl basin, doubles as a dressing table. Bottles and cosmetics are seamlessly concealed behind a slim mirrored cupboard.**

THIS PICTURE: **If you've chosen twin counter-sunk basins for a streamlined look, don't spoil the appearance by cluttering the worktop. Keep out only daily essentials in good-looking containers, such as stainless-steel beakers, and store everything else in a cupboard elsewhere.**

doors or an open shelf below. These are generally floor- rather than wall-mounted. Where funds allow, it's worth investing in custom-built cupboards. Plan the design, and how you will use the interior, as you would fitted kitchen cupboards. You might include extras such as a pull-out waste or laundry bin, or door-mounted wire compartments. For a twin vanity unit, tailor the storage to suit both your needs – lots of drawers for you, and a single door for him.

For a very streamlined look, avoid cupboards and instead equip a thick stone or hardwood worktop with a hanging towel rail. One or two matching shelves below, or a simple open cube design, will look good. Free space underneath the worktop can hold a stack of rattan or steel boxes. Wall-mount extras that might clutter the worktop: try smart stainless-steel containers for soap and cotton wool.

STORING TOWELS

We've all become so obsessed with washing that the lone towel rail is no longer enough. Added to that, many of us love the fresh-towel culture of the gym or spa, and enjoy the look of piled-up towels waiting to be used. For daily storage, you can't beat a heated towel rail. In a modern bathroom, choose a sleek wall-mounted design or, in a period property, a traditional floor-mounted version. Check the size and thickness of your towels before choosing. Some rails have narrow bars, making it tricky to squeeze on a jumbo version or multiple towels in a family bathroom. If you need lots of capacity, invest in a floor-to-ceiling ladder rail, or twin rails. If wall space is limited, a combined radiator/rail is a good solution.

ABOVE LEFT: **Learn a style tip or two from small hotel bathrooms, where extra towels are often stacked onto a smart metal rack close to the bath or shower. These shelves are best reserved for smaller hand towels, while bath towels are better hung on hooks. If white towels are on display, keep them looking pristine.**

ABOVE RIGHT: **It's vital to decide on the type and location of towel rails right at the beginning, so that the plumbing and/or electrics can be sorted out prior to decoration or tiling. The advantage of an electric towel rail is that it can be switched off when not required.**

RIGHT: **In a home lucky enough to boast a sauna or steam room, add a small relaxation area, with lots of shelves for towels.**

CENTRE AND BELOW: **If you like the folded-towel look, reserve it for clean towels, rather than those in use. Wet towels need to be dried on a heated rail, or hung on hooks to air.**

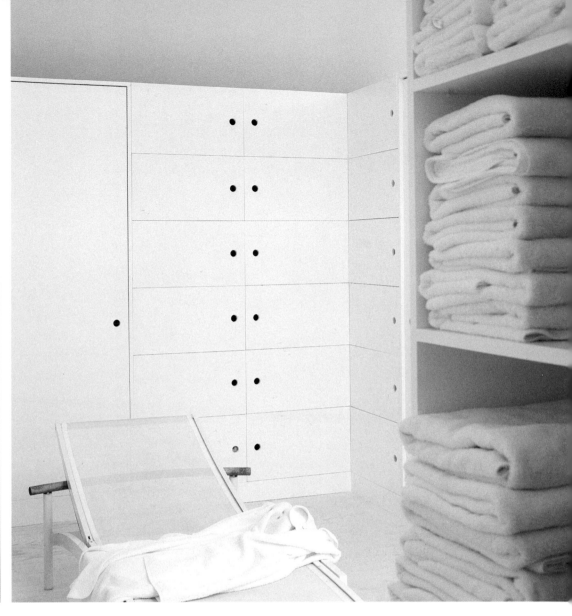

Extra towels can be neatly stacked on fitted open shelves or inside a cupboard, if you have the space. To keep them well aired, consider slatted wooden shelves, or pile them into deep wire drawers. In a small bathroom or a walk-in shower (on a wall away from the water jets), a sturdy wall-mounted shelf, in stainless steel or wood, is great for stashing extra towels. Other unobtrusive solutions include multiple-arm racks, either plain wood or heated metal rails, which push back flat against the wall, or plain towel rings. A steel towel rail, mounted on the front of a basin worktop, or a purpose-built metal basin stand with integral towel rail, provides extra capacity for hand towels. For the truly minimally minded, a row of hooks, close to the shower and mounted high off the floor, is the place to hang up big bath towels.

SOLUTIONS FOR SMALL BATHROOMS

The real challenge in a small bathroom is not necessarily to add more storage, but to create a streamlined space that feels bigger than it really is. In an ideal world, if you have a tiny bathroom that doesn't suit your needs, start again. It needn't involve a huge investment. Armed with your to-scale floor plan, decide what fittings are really necessary. For example, a bath may be removed in favour of a shower, or the hot-water tank sited elsewhere, freeing up precious space. Is a shower really necessary in the family bathroom? Perhaps it could be added elsewhere, such as in a utility room.

Many bathroom suppliers offer sanitary ware for small spaces, so do your research. Options include corner or cloakroom-size basins, and sitz- (hip) baths or corner baths. Wall-mounted sanitary ware not only frees floor space but looks streamlined, so makes the space feel bigger. Flush bathroom fittings have a similar effect. Wall-mounting storage – or slotting it into available alcoves – is desirable. Even the tiniest bathroom has space for a slim, shallow medicine cabinet or an eye-level shelf running around the perimeter of the room. With research, you'll find space-saving extras. Look out for floor-to-ceiling mirror units that conceal revolving shelves, a mirror on a stand equipped with towel rail and shaving shelf, or designs with a hanging rail behind.

The ultimate aim is to strip the amount you must store to the absolute essentials and keep surfaces free from mess. So add securely fixed wall hooks to hold everything from bathroom robes to a fabric laundry bag. Alternatively, add a steel rail (similar to a kitchen utensil rail) across a splashback, and hang up metal or plastic boxes filled with toiletries.

ABOVE: **Early planning meant that this tiny bathroom, in the eaves, could be fitted with deep niches for baskets, to store toilet paper and toiletries. A butler's sink, balanced on a worktop and slim legs, enhances, rather than crowds, the small space.**

LEFT: **Everything in this small bathroom has been cleverly scaled down, yet it is still user-friendly. Lots of shallow drawers keep clutter well ordered, while the integral basin towel rails are just wide enough to hold a hand towel either side.**

THIS PAGE: **If a built-in cupboard
makes a small bathroom feel even
more cramped, design the doors to
include a couple of shallow display
niches, to break up the expanse.
Pale, reflective surfaces – such as
gloss paint or a lacquer finish –
contribute to a feeling of space.**

BATHROOM CHECKLISTS

ITEMS TO ACCOMMODATE

Towels, bath mats, dressing gowns

Spare loo roll, cotton wool, etc.

Cosmetics and toiletries

Cleaning materials

Laundry bin

Medicine cabinet

Daily equipment such as toothbrushes

ISSUES TO ADDRESS

- If the bathroom is small, are there available niches into which built-in storage may be squeezed?
- What is the style – do you want sleek built-in storage to match minimalist choices or a country, unfitted look?
- Can towels be housed elsewhere – for example, in an airing cupboard?
- How many people will use the room – all the family, or is it a master bedroom en suite?

CHILDREN'S ROOMS

THIS PAGE: **This brilliantly designed toddler's room provides safe, dual-purpose storage. While deep under-bed drawers store extra bedding and clothes (and can be made safe from little fingers using childproof catches), low-level open shelves make toys and books accessible for a small child. Maximum use has been made of the lofty ceilings by including high shelves, to keep grown-up books well out of reach.**

ASSESSING SPACE AND LIFESTYLE

A child's room is often the last place we're prepared to spend money. Yet from babyhood children amass quantities of clothes and toys, and need somewhere to store it all. Children's rooms are often small, perhaps shared with siblings, so space pressures build. Kids need to play on the floor and run around, so they deserve a room unencumbered by clutter. They – and you – also need storage that is easy to access, and positively promotes quick tidy-ups.

So take a long, cool look at the children's rooms and the living rooms. Use the checklists at the end of the chapter to create a list for each child. Categorize essentials that must stay in the bedroom (clothes, books, favourite toys), and kit that can go elsewhere. Can most toys be accommodated within capacious kitchen storage or a designated play area? Could sports kit go in a hall cupboard, board games in the living room? With pressure eased in

ABOVE RIGHT: **When all toys must be stored in a bedroom, it's a good idea to hide stacked crates behind sliding doors. Not only can mess be concealed easily, but at night a child will sleep more peacefully if the toys are tucked away.**

RIGHT: **Some children will want to be actively involved in the planning, and decorating, of storage. If they are old enough to understand, ask them what they would like. A junk-shop shelf unit can be painted together. If kids have storage they feel proud of, they are more likely to use it and keep things neat.**

the bedroom, there's a better chance of creating a user-friendly storage system to grow with each child.

The number of children, and their ages, must come into the equation. A young family needs low-level storage, with open shelves, pull-out boxes and fun decorative themes. Older kids will have different needs, and prefer to keep favourite things in their bedrooms. Match a storage system to the planned activity in each room. A designated playroom, for example, requires floor-to-ceiling fitted cupboards to allow lots of free floor space. By contrast, book- and display shelves in a bedroom should be close to the bed. What is the storage personality of each child? Some children respond better to stacking on shelves, while others go for open crates.

VARYING STORAGE OPTIONS

The best-planned storage provides a mix of options including shelves, drawers, cupboards and baskets. Yet the choosing of a design needs a different emphasis to adult storage. First, look at practicalities: focus on floor- to mid-level furniture heights, ease of use (drawers that run smoothly, handles that are simple to grab) and durable finishes. How shelves and cupboards are arranged inside is crucial, as kids' things – from toy soldiers to dolly clothes – need to be well ordered within containers. Include an element of fun. Steer clear of themed items and concentrate on 'secret' panel doors, tiered open cubes to climb up or on, and anything on castors.

Fitted furniture is an excellent choice, particularly in small or attic bedrooms, as every bit of space can be utilized. A built-in single bed can incorporate a book niche in the bedhead, or drawers underneath. For older children a platform bed with a desk below is ideal. One wall devoted to storage, comprising open shelves for display and a floor-to-ceiling cupboard for toys and clothes, gives a neater finish. It's also easier for children to access, and tidy away, things in just one zone. Experiment decoratively with surfaces. Paint MDF shelves in zany colours, or add blackboard panels to cupboard doors.

There is plenty of imaginative children's furniture, but do pick and choose. Bypass scaled-down trunks and wardrobes, as kids will grow out of them in a trice. Far better to invest in an adult-size chest of drawers and a proper single bed with pull-out drawers – in a classic design – that will endure to the teenage years. Mix in funky extras. A metal locker, shelf unit with colourful canvas containers or bench seating with lift-up lid are all practical yet fun.

ABOVE: **In a shared bedroom, it can make sense to invest in one giant chest of drawers. Children may enjoy having their individual drawers labelled.**

ABOVE LEFT: **Think laterally and consider how you might adapt 'adult' storage for kids. A traditional open-shelf unit, designed to stand vertically, provides fantastic floor-level storage for little people.**

BELOW LEFT: **Teenagers will be happy with the tiniest room, if it guarantees them privacy. Customized storage will help ease the space pressure. This platform bed has plenty of drawers for clothes, while a wall-mounted unit keeps the TV at convenient eye level.**

OPPOSITE: **Functional yet fun, this stepped open-shelf unit has generous compartments to hold a variety of storage boxes and sports kit.**

THIS PAGE: **Compartmentalized bookshelves, at a convenient height, are more user-friendly than one long shelf, from which books will easily topple. Custom-made shelves can be tailored in a mix of heights, to accommodate big picture books, reading books and tiny baby books. Adjustable shelves are even better, as when children get older the large books will be replaced with school textbooks and paperbacks.**

OPPOSITE: **As well as clothes, pegs can be used to store backpacks, sports equipment (including swimming costumes and goggles) and coats. Invest in sturdy hooks and fix them securely to the wall. Allow sufficient space in between pegs, so things don't get dislodged easily.**

FLOOR, '

We may

if they a

can set

hangin

keepin

the mo

a lot o

baske

decor

for ho

consi

crate

Choc

In

chil

may

is tl

sor

an

to

th

narrow shelf running the length

several shallow, open cubes, as well as more
traditional wood or metal tiered-shelf units. A wall-
mounted pinboard, either traditional cork with
drawing pins or powder-coated steel with magnets,
is the perfect place to show off photographs, school
certificates and artwork.

When planning clothes storage, younger children
won't need lots of wardrobe hanging space. You can
get away with one low rail for little dresses or jackets,
with jumpers, shorts and tops folded into drawers or
on shelves. Yet every room should be provided with
an array of individual hooks. There are some funky

and fun designs on the market, from metal heart
shapes to traditional painted wooden pegrails.
Situate them low down, according to the height of
your child. On these, kids can hang not just PJs
and dressing gowns, but – if you add a couple of
hangers – school uniform ready for the next day.

STORAGE TO GROW

When children are small it's hard to imagine that they will ever turn into teenagers, yet that time passes with amazing speed. A well-planned storage system can develop with the child, and – with minor adaptations – will still please a decade later. It must also cope with an ever-increasing number of possessions. For this reason, it's a good idea to stick to fairly classic designs. Small decorative changes, such as adding different handles or a wood or MDF surface that can be repainted, are easy to make. Choosing a simple modular system that can be added to year by year is also a good choice.

If you're planning to invest in bespoke storage, try to anticipate more grown-up needs. As school progresses, children need a desktop, a nearby bookshelf and a surface deep enough to hold a computer. In the early years, this can be used as display space, or for painting or drawing, later

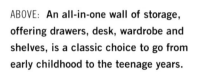

ABOVE: **An all-in-one wall of storage, offering drawers, desk, wardrobe and shelves, is a classic choice to go from early childhood to the teenage years.**

LEFT AND CENTRE: **All children love the idea of a theme bedroom, yet it must be cleverly planned to endure. This nautically inspired design is built to last. The mural is simple and bold, rather than cute, and the built-in drawers and stepped access provide a hint of sophistication.**

FAR LEFT: **Kids' furniture can take a battering. Rather than risk tired-looking finishes in later years, source vintage furniture that has already acquired a charmingly aged patina.**

graduating to the homework zone. The internal fit-out of a full-size wardrobe will also need to adapt. A child of ten and upwards will need more shelf space and a higher hanging rail. Fit shelves on an adjustable system and, as years pass, toy crates can be removed and accessories and shoes added in. As kids get older, more sophisticated extras can replace toy storage systems. A stainless-steel drawer unit on wheels or a bright lacquered TV trolley will instantly upgrade a child's room to a teenager's den.

CHILDREN'S ROOM CHECKLISTS

ITEMS TO ACCOMMODATE

LARGE ITEMS
Futons and sleeping bags
Trucks, dolly equipment, etc.
Pop-up tent
Beanbags and/or small table and chairs
Musical instruments
Doll's house or castle

SMALL ITEMS
Books and games
Toy soldiers, dolly clothes, cars, etc.
Bedside clock, tape recorder
Paper, pens, paints, modelling clay
Soft toys and dolls

CLOTHING AND EQUIPMENT
Hanging space for dresses/smart clothes
Folded tops and trousers
Shoes and boots
Out-of-season clothes
Football/tennis rackets
Ballet or sports kit

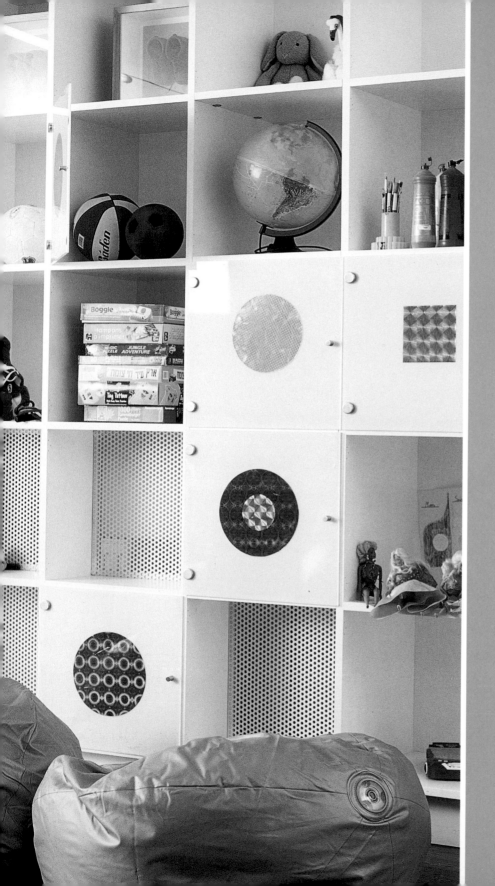

ISSUES TO ADDRESS

- Do all the children's toys need to be incorporated into the bedroom, or can some go into a playroom?
- Think about planning child-height storage, so they can access items by themselves.
- Do you want a flush, streamlined look or a variety of floor baskets and boxes?
- What is the budget, and how can you plan storage to grow with your child(ren)'s needs?
- Are there awkward corners that can accommodate built-in storage?
- How will you incorporate display space?

HALLS, LANDINGS AND STAIRS

ABOVE: Match built-in cupboards to the existing stair architecture. Traditional homes will need plain panelled and painted doors, whereas in this modern home minimalist flush doors and simple handles complement the steel rail.

RIGHT: If adding wardrobes to a landing, ensure there's sufficient room to open the doors; sliding panels take up less space than conventional doors. Insert light-refracting materials, from clear or frosted glass to mesh or chicken wire, to lighten the look.

DEAD SPACE STORAGE

The beauty of compiling a whole-home assessment right at the beginning is that spare space quickly becomes apparent. As you sort individual rooms, every centimetre will be accounted for, but what about 'dead' areas? Look at halls and stairs with fresh eyes. Most of us struggle with tiny proportions, but there is always potential! At the same time, refer to your checklists to see what items haven't yet found a home. Some are daily essentials – for example, bikes and buggies – so need to be near the hall. Infrequently used items, from surfboards to toolboxes, may be stored in less accessible spots.

In a period home, the cavity beneath the first flight of stairs has rich potential. Suit the type of storage to the area. An entrance hall will require smart built-in cupboards, whereas in a basement kitchen a grid of open shelves and baskets is useful. Beneath a new flight of stairs from a bedroom landing to a loft conversion, create a linen cupboard by adding slatted wooden shelves. We don't all want fitted storage. A relaxed approach in a country home might be to add a tall chest of drawers to the space, just the place to hold out-of-season clothes.

Landings and halls are also rich in potential. If it is blessed with wide proportions, a bedroom landing might be the spot for a trunk stashed with sleeping bags, or in the hall add a console with drawers for stationery and stamps. Only add a piece of furniture if there's room for everyone to bypass it easily. Where space is tight, fitted options are a better idea. Can you 'steal' the depth of a paperback book, to build in a floor-to-ceiling bookshelf on a landing, or line one wall of a long, thin hall with fitted cupboards to conceal coats, shoes and bags?

LEFT: **If the master bedroom is small, a top-floor landing just outside can be converted into a mini dressing room. Add mirrored doors to a bank of wardrobes.**

FAR LEFT: **An open-plan loft lacks lots of 'spare' walls for adding shelves, so consider creating a hallway using a floor-to-ceiling storage unit. Lined with a mix of cupboards and bookshelves, this one adds a dash of homely character to the industrial space. Units such as these don't need to be custom-made. Many shops, from designer stores to high-street sources, offer modular storage systems with a mix of cupboards and open shelves, which can be used to create varied looks. They are ideal for use in high-traffic areas.**

DECORATIVE STORAGE IN HIGH-TRAFFIC AREAS

We spend lots of time traipsing up and down the hall
and stairs, but often this is the last place we look
when devising decorative solutions. Yet traffic areas
make fantastic gallery spaces. Paint walls a good
neutral or a deep colour and add low-voltage lighting.
Do you have a treasured collection to display? Is it
better wall-mounted or stacked at low level? Think
of everyday objects that need to be accessible, but
which will look eye-catching if grouped attractively.
It's amazing what looks good en masse, from rows
of colourful trainers to stacks of old *Beano* comics.

Many precious or multiple items are best arranged
on shelves, so look for niches at the turn of the stair,

ABOVE LEFT: **Alcove storage for books and magazines is a great stairway choice. The reading material is still accessible, yet looks attractive arranged in stacks. Experiment with the style of display. Long shelves look good broken up with a mix of horizontal and vertical piles, and a haphazard finish looks relaxed.**

ABOVE RIGHT: **Pay attention to the style of shelves in an entrance hall, as they are the first thing a visitor sees. Beautiful wood veneers, or a dark paint colour, are sophisticated.**

RIGHT: **Carefully framed, mundane items, even firewood, look good.**

OPPOSITE: **Consider using a self-assembly budget storage unit to fill a deep niche, as only the front façade will be on show. This cleverly planned landing combines a show-off row of shoes with a grid of baskets for less attractive items.**

on a landing or either side of a doorway. If planning built-in shelves or criss-cross compartments, measure key items first, so storage looks tailored. (If the collection is still growing, add extra space now.) Think of the items as abstracts, and arrange them symmetrically for the best effect. Use lighting to draw attention, especially in a dark corridor or on the stairs at night. Consider spotlights, under-shelf lighting or coloured lights to highlight niches.

Wall-mounted collections look so good on stairs because you get the advantage of a double-height wall, and special collections add personality to a hall, which is vital for first impressions. Differentiate between a permanent collection (from straw hats to antique tennis rackets), which can be hung up high on conventional picture hooks, and things you want to show off, but need to access. A cool collection of skateboards or designer handbags can be displayed lower down on wall brackets or cup hooks, then removed when you need one.

PLANNING CUPBOARDS

Where there is ample room in one or more traffic areas, then it makes sense to add a run of floor-to-ceiling cupboards. If the space is on the ground floor, near the back door, such storage can take the place of a conventional boot room, holding outdoor gear, Wellingtons and gardening kit. Upstairs landing cupboards are the best place for spare bedding, or toy storage, if close to the kids' rooms. Avoid putting fitted cupboards in an entrance hall, as they will dominate the space. Instead, run them down one side of a corridor, or 'borrow' space from a room adjacent to the hall and create a walk-in cloakroom.

It's important to get the style right, so a bank of cupboards doesn't cramp proportions. Think about scale. Foreshortening dimensions, so there's a clear gap between the top of the wardrobe and the ceiling, promotes a sense of spaciousness. Likewise, a wall-mounted cupboard that stops short of the floor seems less bulky. Consider door styles. In a modern setting, flush doors painted to match the walls will all but disappear. By contrast, in a low-ceilinged space, lots of slim doors will draw the eye upwards and contribute to a sense of height. Mirrored, clear or sand-blasted glass, or glossy lacquered doors, all reflect light and improve proportions.

Approach internal cupboard organization with the same precision you would for bedroom wardrobes. A 'cloakroom' cupboard should be fitted with wire drawers for sorting gloves, hats and scarves, shoe racks and hanging space for coats. Include a full-length mirror on the inside of one door, and small baskets for extras like a clothes brush, hairbrushes and hair ties for kids, and a shoe-cleaning kit. Then no one has an excuse to go out looking a mess.

ABOVE: **In a corridor with high ceilings, these cupboards have been designed with niche bookshelves above. Good lighting is crucial in a dark corridor. Here, a ceiling spotlight has been added to highlight the books decoratively. But also fit the insides of cupboards with an automatic light, so that they are illuminated when the doors open. If in doubt, visit a lighting showroom for ideas, or – if you've planned a lot of built-in cupboards – hire a lighting consultant to advise on the entire project.**

OPPOSITE: **Adding built-in cupboards is a great way to square off an awkward corner in a hall. If there are other features in the way, such as a radiator, then build that into the design using a radiator grille.**

BELOW: **Most apartments feature several corridors and – provided there is still space to pass up and down them – lining such spaces with cupboards is a clever way to incorporate storage. For a seamless finish, take doors floor to ceiling, without a skirting or cornice, and add touch-catches or very minimal handles. If you are decorating on a budget, it's not essential to spend a fortune on custom-made cupboards. Many high-street stores and DIY shops have a great selection of self-assembly furniture, or consider using a shop-bought cupboard carcass and adding personalized doors.**

LEFT: **In a busy family hall, provide low hooks for children's coats, as well as a conventional coat rack. If baseball bats and tennis rackets are in constant use, stow them in a wide umbrella stand; group footballs into a wicker or rubber basket.**

RIGHT: **For the ultimate clutter-free hall, utilize under-stairs cupboards for everyday coats and bags, and add hooks inside for keys. Keep a stair basket on the bottom step, so items needing to go upstairs are contained.**

FAR RIGHT: **A low cabinet with drawers and a small cupboard offers a traditional solution in a country hall.**

ORGANIZING THE HALL

Given its high frequency of use, the hall deserves extra-special attention. We all tend to dump bags and coats on arrival, there may be bikes to store as well as post, and so on. If everything has its place, household members can be expected to tidy up, and visitors won't be confronted with mess. Most halls are small, so unless things are safely stowed accidents will happen. Think of the rush in which most of us leave home. If the hall is disorganized, finding keys or a mobile takes twice as long.

First, sort out the wheeled things, as these can be a source of major disturbance. While a folded-up buggy may be hung on a wall hook or stashed into a wide umbrella stand, a bike can be fitted onto a sturdy wall rack. Alternatively, devise a pulley system using yacht fittings, to store it near the ceiling. The beauty of modern scooters is that they can be folded up, so make sure they're tucked into

a cupboard. Skateboards can be drilled with a small hole and suspended from a large cup hook, and rollerblades hung on hooks, using their laces.

To organize everyday coats and bags only (any more, and the hall will look a mess), supply either a traditional coatstand or a chic wall-mounted pegrail. Look out for slim pieces of furniture to add. A bench with a lift-up lid, or a dresser with cupboards beneath, is ideal for stowing bags, or try a console table with a large wicker basket tucked underneath. For umbrellas, add a smart leather, wicker or steel umbrella stand.

Every hall needs a safe place for the little things, such as loose change, keys and post. If there's room, a tabletop with a few open baskets will keep essentials in order, though keep them sufficiently far away from the front door so that thieves can't access keys. In a small hall, a wall-mounted set of pigeonholes for post and a smart metal key cupboard will do the trick.

HALL, LANDING AND STAIRS CHECKLISTS

ITEMS TO ACCOMMODATE

LARGE ITEMS
Coats, scarves, hats, etc.

Boots and outdoor shoes

Bags

Vacuum cleaner and brush

SMALL ITEMS
Phone and phone directories

Post and stamps

Keys and mobile phones

Pencils and notepad

WHEELED ITEMS
Pushbikes and scooter

Baby buggy, rollerblades and
  skateboards

DECORATIVE ITEMS
Books and magazines

Paintings and collections

Clock

ISSUES TO ADDRESS

- How wide and/or spacious is the hall and/or corridors? Will adding extra storage impede human traffic flow and ruin proportions?
- Can built-in storage (e.g. bookshelves) be employed to add interest to traffic areas?
- Think about dual-purpose furniture such as a narrow bench with a lift-up lid.
- Consider the potential for wall-mounting items such as bike racks or shoe racks.

SOURCE DIRECTORY

BOXES AND BASKETS

The Empty Box Company
The Old Dairy
Coomb Farm Building
Balchins Lane
Westcott, Nr Dorking
Surrey RH4 3LW
01306 740193
www.emptybox.co.uk
Paper-covered decorative boxes made to order, including large wedding-dress size, hat- and shoeboxes, DVD and photo boxes, plus storage files. They will also cover in your own fabric as a bespoke service.

The Holding Company
241–245 King's Road
London SW3 5EL
020 7352 1600
www.theholdingcompany.co.uk
Comprehensive range of baskets and boxes from CD holders to stair baskets, in every finish from leather and see-through plastic to rattan and metal. Specialist clothes storage includes zip-up wardrobes, shoe- and hatboxes and drawer organizers.

Muji
187 Oxford Street
London W1R 1AJ
020 7437 7503
www.muji.co.uk
Acrylic, cardboard and polypropylene storage boxes in many sizes, plus free-standing aluminium shelves and beds with under-bed drawers.

Oka Direct
The Coachworks
80 Parsons Green Lane
London SW6 4HU
0870 1606002
www.okadirect.com
Inspired collection of attractive rattan baskets in many shapes, plus useful extras such as umbrella stands, trunks, log baskets and CD boxes.

INTERNAL CUPBOARD FITTINGS

Hafele
Swift Valley Industrial Estate
Rugby, Warwickshire CV21 1RD
01788 542020
www.hafele.co.uk
Wonderful selection of internal fittings for cupboards including pull-out wire drawers, shoe and clothing racks, hanging rails, hooks and trouser presses.

Nu-Line
315 Westbourne Park Road
London W11 1EF
020 7727 7748
www.nu-line.net
A good choice of useful internal wardrobe fittings from drawers to hanging rails, plus pull-out bins to corner carousels for kitchens, and bathroom accessories from shelves to trolleys.

TV AND HI-FI STORAGE

Dixons
0870 850333
www.dixons.co.uk
Useful and good-looking selection of modern metal and glass TV and DVD stands and media storage systems.

Gibson Music
Unit 8, The Broomhouse
50 Sulivan Road
London SW6 3DX
020 7384 2270
www.gibson-music.com
Specialists in home entertainment systems who will also design fitted furniture to incorporate the technology, in any bespoke finish to match your scheme.

John Lewis
300 Oxford Street
London W1A 1EX
020 7629 7711
www.johnlewis.com
Comprehensive range of TV stands in glass, metal and wood, plus TV wall kits, speaker stands and cable-management systems.

FREE-STANDING FURNITURE

B & Q
0845 2221000 for nearest store
www.diy.co.uk
Wide variety of inexpensive storage from free-standing shelf units and kitchen trolleys to fitted and unfitted bedroom furniture and stacking storage boxes.

Cargo Home Shop
209 Tottenham Court Road
London W1P 9AF
020 7580 2895
www.cargohomeshop.com
Excellent selection of budget free-standing shelf units in finishes from wood to glass, plus useful cabinets and sideboards.

The Conran Shop
89 Fulham Road
London SW3 6RD
020 7589 7401
www.conran.com
Beautifully designed range of modern furniture for every room, plus an excellent selection of storage boxes and baskets.

Habitat
0845 6010740 for nearest store
www.habitat.net
Modern, sleek selection of wardrobes, free-standing shelves, office storage and modular storage units, plus inexpensive ever-changing selection of cardboard, wicker and plastic containers.

Heal's
196 Tottenham Court Road
London W1T 7LQ
020 7636 1666
www.heals.co.uk
Quality, contemporary furniture in a range of options from wardrobes and chests of drawers to sideboards and home-office storage systems.

Laura Ashley
0871 2302301
www.lauraashley.com
Stylish selection of cabinets, armoires, sideboards and more, plus an excellent version of an oak plan chest and glamorous Thirties-style mirrored furniture, including a dressing table and a chest of drawers.

Marks & Spencer
0845 6031603
www.marksandspencer.com
Bookcases, armoires, chests and cabinets in a mix of styles from Shaker to modern and sleek, plus useful kitchen extras such as a butcher's block on wheels.

The Pier
0845 6091234
www.pier.co.uk
Traditional but well-priced selection of furniture in dark stained wood and rattan, including Chinese chest TV cabinets and multi-media units, cupboard-style work units, bookshelves, wardrobes and chests of drawers.

CHILDREN'S STORAGE

Chic Shack
77 Lower Richmond Road
London SW15 1ET
020 8785 7777
www.chicshack.net
Very pretty selection of children's painted furniture, including single beds with storage drawers, toy chests, glass-fronted chests of drawers, shelf units, bedside tables and dressing tables.

The Children's Furniture Company
020 7737 7303
www.thechildrensfurniturecompany.com
Well-made and co-ordinated range of children's furniture including chests of drawers, wall-mounted shelves, toy boxes and matching beds in hardwood, with ash interchangeable coloured panels.

The Great Little Trading Company
0870 8506000
www.gltc.co.uk
Useful mail-order catalogue packed with toy chests, storage boxes and baskets, peg racks and hooks and decorative shelves. Plus good range of free-standing furniture in different themes and colours, from metal lockers to beds with under-bed storage.

The Little White Company
261 Pavilion Road
London SW1X 0BP
0870 9009555
www.thewhitecompany.com
Mail-order company and chain of shops with a range of white-painted kids' furniture including blanket boxes, junior wardrobes and shelves, plus gingham-covered storage boxes and linen baskets.

Mothercare
08453 304030
www.mothercare.com
Good basic range of nursery furniture including chests of drawers, blanket boxes and peg shelves, in a mix of wood or white finishes.

Wigwam Kids
0870 9027500
www.wigwamkids.co.uk
Lovely selection of children's free-standing furniture, including unusual storage like boat storage trunks, plus useful and attractive hooks and wall-mounted shelves.

Woolworths
0845 6081100
www.woolworths.co.uk
Basic but attractive storage boxes and bags, hooks and peg rails in fun colours and jolly motifs.

MODULAR STORAGE

Aram
110 Drury Lane
London WC2B 5SG
020 7557 7557
www.aram.co.uk
Designer modular storage systems plus inspired desk systems and wheeled trolleys, from a choice of European designers.

BO Concept
158 Tottenham Court Road
London W1T 7NH
020 7388 2447
www.boconcept.co.uk
Smart, modular systems for living rooms, dining rooms and bedrooms in a wide range of wood veneers and glass. Plus modern free-standing furniture, from chests of drawers to sideboards, and a good selection of TV and hi-fi units.

Purves and Purves
222 Tottenham Court Road
London W1T 7PZ
020 7580 8223
www.purves.co.uk
Lots of modern storage options including modular units in wood, glass and steel, plus desks, perspex tables and magazine racks and bedroom and living-room furniture.

Viaduct
1–10 Summers Street
London EC1R 5BD
020 7278 8456
www.viaduct.co.uk
Excellent selection of modular storage units by leading European designers, plus free-standing modern furniture for living rooms, bedrooms and home offices.

FITTED STORAGE SYSTEMS

California Closets
Unit 8
Staples Corner Business Park
1000 North Circular Road
London NW2 7JP
020 8208 4544
www.californiaclosets.co.uk
Fitted home-storage systems for bedrooms, garages, home offices and laundry rooms, in a range of finishes and with useful extras such as pull-out bins, shelves, hanging rails and more.

Espacio
276 King's Road
London SW3 5AW
020 7376 5088
www.espacio.co.uk
Comprehensive stock of modern European furniture, including the Italian Mobileffe range of fitted and open-plan wardrobes in 24 coloured lacquer finishes and wood.

IKEA
0845 3551141
www.IKEA.co.uk
Inexpensive free-standing and fitted furniture systems to mix and match including an aluminium, steel and white lacquer version. Also internal fittings such as shoe racks, clothes rails and trouser hangers. Doors in finishes including lacquer, wood or mirror.

Magnet
01325 744355
www.magnet.co.uk
Sleek, well-priced range of fitted kitchens, bedroom cupboards and office furniture, in a range of finishes from wood veneer to glass and white, with large range of extras, such as shoe racks, pull-out baskets, plate racks and pull-out shelves.

CUSTOM-MADE SHELVES AND CUPBOARDS

Charles Codrington Creative Wood
17 Trent Road
London SW2 5BJ
07930 406610
Streamlined bespoke cabinets in a choice of woods, or ready-to-paint MDF.

Charles Hurst Workshop
Unit 21
Bow Triangle Business Centre
Eleanor Street
London E3 4NP
020 8981 8562
Well-proportioned and simply styled architectural joinery.

Dominic Ash
020 7689 0676
www.dominicash.co.uk
Bespoke joinery in simple contemporary styles and a choice of hardwoods.

BATHROOM STORAGE

Colourwash
63–65 Fulham High Street
London SW6 3JJ
020 7371 0911
www.colourwash.co.uk
A good selection of modern vanity unit storage options, plus shelves, trolleys and cabinets.

Homebase
0845 0778888 for nearest store
www.homebase.co.uk
Excellent choice of well-priced chrome and glass shelves, wood vanity units including a corner version, cabinets and free-standing shelf units.

Ocean
0870 2426283
www.oceanuk.com
Mail-order catalogue with really smart selection of modern bathroom storage including chrome and glass shelves, stainless-steel mobile cabinets, vanity units and revolving slimline storage units.

Vogue UK
0870 4030111
www.vogue-uk.com
Heated towel rails and radiator/towel rails in every style from ladder to floor-standing.

West One Bathrooms
45–46 South Audley Street
London W1K 2PY
020 7499 1845
www.westonebathrooms.com
Designer basins with vanity units or on stands, slick chrome accessories including wall-mounted soap dispensers and towel rails.

OFFICE STORAGE

Paperchase
213 Tottenham Court Road
London W1T 7PS
020 7467 6200
www.paperchase.co.uk
Inspiring and wide selection of stationery and desk accessories including files, pen pots and storage boxes, in many colours and ever-changing styles.

Ryman
0800 801901
www.ryman.co.uk
High-street chain with good office storage including mobile computer trolleys, cabinets, filing cabinets and stacking storage boxes.

Viking Direct
0800 1971747
www.viking-direct.co.uk
Wide selection of basic office equipment including classic filing cabinets, bookshelves and desks, plus desk accessories and every type of file. Also smart metal lockers suitable for use in the hall.

MAIL ORDER

Baileys By Mail
The Engine Shed
Station Approach
Ross-on-Wye
Herefordshire HR9 7BW
01989 561931
www.baileyshomeandgarden.com
Mail-order catalogue full of utility and antique extras from wire baskets and traditional folding clothes airers to a selection of leather trunks, seed trays and storage crates.

Cath Kidston
020 7229 8000
www.cathkidston.co.uk
Shops and mail-order catalogue with pretty selection of carrier and picnic bags, decorative box files and laundry items like peg bags and laundry bags, all in retro florals or spots.

Cucina Direct
0870 4204300
www.cucinadirect.co.uk
Mail-order catalogue with selection of kitchen storage from bread bins to biscuit tins, plus storage boxes, vegetable trolleys and laundry essentials such as foldaway drying racks and wall-mounted clothes driers.

Lakeland
015394 88100
www.lakelandlimited.co.uk
Fabulously useful selection of stacking boxes and crates, space-saving solutions like pull-out laundry racks, trolleys on wheels and wall hooks.

DECORATIVE SMALL STORAGE

Bombay Duck
020 8749 3000
www.bombayduck.co.uk
Pretty range of single and double decorative hooks including coloured glass, metal hearts and children's motifs, plus aluminium and glass cupboard-door knobs.

Dibor
0870 0133666
www.dibor.co.uk
Mail-order company with a French bias, including pretty extras such as willow storage chests and log baskets, stair baskets, under-bed trays and a wood shoe-cleaning box. Also a range of pretty painted country bedroom furniture, plus metal hooks, boot tidies and magazine racks.

The French House
0870 9014547
www.thefrenchhouse.net
Mail-order catalogue with attractive French accessories. Stock includes a selection of willow baskets, brass coat racks, wireware baskets and period-style porcelain bathroom soap dishes, towel rails and hooks, plus a pretty solid wood medicine cabinet.

Graham and Green
4–10 Elgin Crescent
London W11 2HX
0845 1306622
www.grahamandgreen.co.uk
Decorative home accessories with an eclectic range of storage items including magazine racks, pretty hooks, mirror jewellery boxes, and bathroom cabinets and trolleys on wheels.

Urban Outfitters
36–38 High Street Kensington
London W8 4PF
020 7761 1001
www.urbn.com
Fun, funky storage boxes, baskets and wall hooks in an ever-changing mix of colours, materials and styles, including good retro designs.

PICTURE CREDITS

27.12 Design Ltd
333 Hudson Street, 10th Floor
New York, NY 10014
+1 212 727 8169
www.2712design.com
Pages 40br, 93l

An Angel At My Table
116A Fortress Road
London NW5 2HL
020 7424 9777
www.angelatmytable.co.uk
Pages 30b, 31br, 36c, 36b

Andrew Treverton
Architect
07799 586810
Pages 72–73, 78–79, 113a

Angela A'Court
Artist
orangedawe@hotmail.com
Pages 98–99

Angela Kearsey Designs
Interior design and decoration
angela.Kearsey@btinternet.com
Endpapers, pages 57a, 128l

Ann-Louise Roswald Ltd
Fashion, textiles and interior design
020 7250 1583
Fax 020 7684 8790
www.annlouiseroswald.com
Page 89ar

Asfour Guzy Architects
594 Broadway
New York, NY 10012
+1 212 334 9350
easfour@asfourguzy.com
Pages 10 inset, 27l, 40ar, 57br, 63, 64, 70bl, 100 inset, 124a

Baileys Home & Garden
The Engine Shed
Station Approach
Ross-on-Wye
Herefordshire HR9 7BW
01989 563015
Fax 01989 768172
www.baileyshomeandgarden.com
Pages 8r, 112r

behun/ziff design
153 East 53rd Street, 43rd Floor
New York, NY 10022
+1 212 292 6233
Fax +1 212 292 6790
Page 107l

Belmont Freeman Architects
110 West 40 Street
New York, NY 10018
+1 212 382 3311
Fax +1 212 730 1229
www.belmontfreeman.com
Page 46b

Bexon Woodhouse Creative
020 8398 2002
create@bexonwoodhouse.com
Page 29l

Bowles & Linares
32 Hereford Road
London W2 5AJ
020 7229 9886
Page 18r

Brian Ayling
Artist
020 8802 9853
Page 38br

Bruce Bierman Design, Inc.
29 West 15 Street
New York, NY 10011
+1 212 243 1935
Fax +1 212 243 6615
www.biermandesign.com
Pages 16–17, 74–75

Charles Bateson Design Consultants
Interior design
18 Kings Road
St Margarets
Twickenham TW1 2QS
Fax 020 8891 6483
charles.bateson@btinternet.com
Page 47a both

Charlotte Crosland Interiors
62 St Mark's Road
London W10 6NN
020 8960 9442
Fax 020 8960 9714
mail@charlottecrosland.com
www.charlottecrosland.com
Pages 128–129, 131b

Christina Wilson
christinawilson@btopenworld.com
Pages 23a, 61l, 101b, 121

Circus Architects
Unit 111 The Foundry
165 Blackfriars Road
London SE1 8EN
020 7953 7322
Fax 020 7953 7255
Pages 122–123, 123l

Clare Mosley
Gilding, eglomisé panels and
mirrors, lamp bases, finials and
curtain accessories
Tel/fax 020 7708 3123
Page 84

Clare Nash
House stylist
020 8742 9991
Pages 68r, 91

Coburn Architecture
45 Main Street, Suite 1210
Brooklyn, NY 11201
+1 718 624 1700
Fax +1 718 624 3232
www.coburnarch.com
Pages 100 main, 113br

cxt sarl d'architecture
Fabienne Couvert & Guillaume
Terver Architectes Associés
12 rue Saint Fiacre
75002 Paris
+33 1 55 34 98 50
Fax +33 1 55 34 98 49
cxtsarl@couvertterver-architectes.com
www.couvertterver-architectes.com
Pages 12–13, 70al, 97a

David Vanderhook
One New Inn Square
020 7729 3645
Page 104ar

Dive Architects
10 Park Street
London SE1 9AB
020 7407 0955
mail@divearchitects.com
www.divearchitects.com
Pages 10–11, 24–25, 92, 103r, 118al

Dols Wong Architects
Loft 3, 329 Harrow Road
London W9 3RB
020 7266 2129
Fax 020 7266 2179
dolswong@btinternet.com
Endpapers, pages 57a, 128l

Dominic Ash Ltd
103 Whitecross Street
London EC1Y 8JD
Tel/fax 020 7689 0676
dominic@dominicash.co.uk
www.dominicash.co.uk
Pages 45r, 118b

Eger Architects
Architects and landscape architects
2 D'eynsford Road
London SE5 7EB
020 7701 6771
Fax 020 7708 5716
design@egerarchitects.com
www.egerarchitects.com
Page 131ar

Elizabeth Alford
60 Thomas Street
New York, NY 10013
+1 212 385 2185
Fax +1 212 385 2186
Page 116

Filip Van Bever
Kitchen design
Filipvanbever@skynet.be
Page 27r

François Muracciole
Architect
54 rue de Montreuil
75011 Paris
+33 1 43 71 33 03
francois.muracciole@libertysurf.fr
Page 42

Granit Chartered Architects Ltd
020 7924 4555
Fax 020 7924 5666
www.granit.co.uk
Pages 22, 93r

Gustavo Martinez Design
206 Fifth Avenue, 4th Floor
New York, NY 10010
+1 212 686 3102
Fax +1 212 686 3104
gmdecor@aol.com
Page 36ar

Guy Hills
Photographer
020 7916 2610
guyhills@hotmail.com
Page 20a

Guy Stansfeld
020 8962 8666
Page 90br

Haifa Hammami
Architect
07730 307612
Pages 41 both, 65, 94–95

Henri Fitzwilliam-Lay
Interior design
hfitz@hotmail.com
Pages 26l, 52

Hilton McConnico
8 rue Antoine Panier
93170 Bagnolet, Paris
Page 103l

HM2 Architects
Architects and designers
33–37 Charterhouse Square
London EC1M 6EA
020 7600 5151
andrew.hanson@harper-mackay.co.uk
Page 107r

Hogarth Architects Ltd
020 7565 8366
info@hogartharchitects.co.uk
www.hogartharchitects.co.uk
Pages 47b, 58–59, 69, 112al, 117a

Hugh Broughton Architects
4 Addison Bridge Place
London W14 8XP
020 7602 8840
Fax 020 7602 5254
www.hbarchitects.co.uk
Page 24a

Interior Concepts
6 Warren Hall
Manor Road
Loughton
Essex IG10 4RP
020 8508 9952
Fax 020 8502 4382
jo_interiorconcepts@hotmail.com
www.jointeriorconcepts.co.uk
Pages 9a, 48–49, 55, 88b

J&M Davidson
Gallery:
97 Golborne Road
London W10 5NL
Shop:
42 Ledbury Road
London W11 2SE
Page 24b

J.O.B. Interieur
Dijkstraat 5
3961 AA Wijk bij Duurstede
The Netherlands
+31 343 578818
Fax +31 343 578157
JOBINT@xs4all.nl
Pages 43 both, 106

Johanne Riss
Stylist, designer and fashion
designer
35 Place du Nouveau Marché
aux Graens
1000 Bruxelles
Belgium
+32 2 51 30 900
Fax +32 2 51 43 284
www.johanneriss.com
Page 109r

John Barman, Inc.
Interior design and decoration
500 Park Avenue
New York, NY 10022
+1 212 838 9443
john@barman.com
www.johnbarman.com
Page 18l

Jonathan Clark Architects
020 7286 5676
Fax 020 7490 8530
jonathan@jonathanclarkarchitects.co.uk
Pages 35, 54, 85b both

Johnson Naylor
13 Britton Street
London EC1M 5SX
020 7490 8885
Fax 020 7490 0038
www.johnsonnaylor.com
Pages 136–137

Josephine Macrander
Interior designer
+31 299 402 804
Fax +31 203 304 084
Page 14

140

Kristiina Ratia Designs
+1 203 852 0027
Pages 11, 21 background

Lena Proudlock
www.lenaproudlock.com
Page 66 both

Marie-Hélène de Taillac
www.mariehelenedetaillac.com
Pages 10 background, 66–67

Malin Iovino Design
Tel/fax 020 7252 3542
07956 326122
iovino@btconnect.com
Page 7

Marino + Giolito
Architecture and interior design
161 West 16th Street
New York, NY 10011
Tel/fax +1 212 675 5737
marino.giolito@rcn.com
Pages 62, 80–81

Mark Kirkley
Designer and manufacturer
of interior metalwork
Tel/fax 01424 812613
Page 135r

Mark Smith
Smithcreative
15 St George's Road
London W4 1AU
020 8747 3909
Fax 020 8742 3902
info@smithcreative.net
Pages 6, 8l, 31ar, 68l, 95, 96al

Michael Nathenson
Unique Environments
Design and architecture
33 Florence Street
London N1 2FW
020 7431 6978
Fax 020 7431 6975
mbn@compuserve.com
www.unique-environments.co.uk
Pages 32–33, 56a

Michael Neumann Architecture
11 East 88th Street
New York, NY 10128
+1 212 828 0407
www.mnarch.com
Pages 38al, 38ar, 70–71b

MOOArc
198 Blackstock Road
London N5 1EN
www.mooarc.com
Page 56b

Mullman Seidman Architects
Architecture and interior design
443 Greenwich Street, # 2A
New York, NY 10013
+1 212 431 0770
Fax +1 212 431 8428
msa@mullmanseidman.com
www.mullmanseidman.com
Pages 12, 21al, 21 inset, 51 both, 60, 90ar, 108l, 110b

Nico Rensch Architeam
www.architeam.co.uk
Pages 50–51, 125

Nicoletta Marazza
via G. Morone, 8
20121 Milano
Tel/fax +39 2 7601 4482
Page 28al

Nigel Smith
Architect
020 7278 8802
n-smith@dircon.co.uk
Page 108r

Orefelt Associates
43 Pall Mall Deposit
124–128 Barlby Road
London W10 6BL
020 8960 2560
Page 109l

Paul Collier, Architect
209 rue St Maur
75010 Paris
+33 1 53 72 49 32
paul.collier@architecte.net
Page 19 insets both

Paul Daly Design Studio Ltd
11 Hoxton Square
London N1 6NU
020 7613 4855
Fax 020 7613 5848
studio@pauldaly.com
www.pauldaly.com
Pages 40l, 61r, 96b

Peter Romaniuk
The Flower House
Cynthia Street
London N1 9JF
020 7837 7373
Page 1

Retrouvius Reclamation
& Design
2A Ravensworth Road
Kensal Green
London NW10 5NR
Tel/fax 020 8960 6060
mail@retrouvius.com
www.retrouvius.com
Page 20a

Roger Oates
London Showroom:
1 Munro Terrace
(off Riley Street)
London SW10 0DL
020 7351 2288
Eastnor Shop:
The Long Barn, Eastnor
Herefordshire HR8 1EL
01531 631611
www.rogeroates.co.uk
Page 112bl

Royal Scandinavia A/S
Designer and architect MAA
Grethe Meyer
Smallegade 45
2000 Frederiksberg
Denmark
+45 38 144 848
Pages 23b, 31l, 34b

Sage and Coombe Architects
205 Hudson Street, Suite 1002
New York, NY 10013
+1 212 226 9600
Fax +1 212 226 8456
www.sageandcoombe.com
Pages 94, 134–135

Sean Kelly Gallery
528 West 29th Street
New York, NY 10001
+1 212 239 1181
Fax +1 212 239 2467
www.skny.com
Page 53

Seth Stein Architects
15 Grand Union Centre
West Row
Ladbroke Grove
London W10 5AS
020 8968 8581
Pages 34ar, 120, 123r

Sheppard Day Design
020 7821 2002
Pages 86–87

Simon Colebrook
Douglas Stephen Partnership
140–142 St John Street
London EC1V 4UB
020 7336 7884
Fax 020 7336 7841
dsp@dspl.co.uk
www.dspl.co.uk
Page 87a

Site Specific Ltd
60a Peartree Street
London EC1V 3SB
020 7490 3176
Fax 020 7490 3427
www.sitespecificltd.co.uk
Page 129l

Sophie Eadie
The New England Shutter
Company
16 Jaggard Way
London SW12 8SG
020 8675 1099
Fax 020 8675 8579
www.tnesc.co.uk
Pages 26r 87b, 108–109

Specht Harpman
338 West 39th Street
New York, NY 10018
+1 212 239 1150
Fax +1 212 239 1180
inquiries@spechtharpman.com
www.spechtharpman.com
Page 132l

Stephen Blatt Architects
10 Danforth Street
Portland, ME 04112-0583
+1 207 761 5911
www.sbarchitects.com
Page 13

Steven Learner Studio
Architecture and interior design
307 Seventh Avenue
New York, NY 10001
+1 212 741 8583
Fax +1 212 741 2180
info@stevenlearnerstudio.com
www.stevenlearnerstudio.com
Page 53

Stickland Coombe
258 Lavender Hill
London SW11 1LJ
020 7924 1699
Fax 020 7585 2201
www.sticklandcoombe.com
Page 81l

Susan Cropper
www.63hlg.com
Pages 96ar, 102, 105

Tessuti
Interiors and fabrics
Doorniksewijk 76
8500 Kortrijk
Belgium
+32 56 25 29 27
info@tessuti.be
www.tessuti.be
Page 27r

The Plot London
Interior design
77 Compton Street
London EC1V 0BN
020 7251 8116
Fax 020 7251 8117
helen@theplotlondon.com
www.theplotlondon.com
Pages 25b, 38bl, 85a

Theis & Khan Architects
22a Bateman's Row
London EC2A 3HH
020 7729 9329
Fax 020 7729 9341
mail@theisandkhan.com
www.theisandkhan.com
Pages 30a, 76–77, 119

Tito Canella
Canella & Achilli Architects
via Revere # 7/9
20123 Milano
+39 2 4695 222
Fax +39 2 4813 704
ac@planet.it
www.canella-achilli.com
Pages 34al, 129r

Tobias Jacobsen
www.tobiasjacobsen.dk
Pages 14–15

Totem Design
Ian Hume
2 Alexander Street
London W2 5NT
020 7243 0692
totem.uk@virgin.net
Pages 26l, 52

Tyler London Ltd
22a Ives Street
London SW3 2ND
020 7581 3677
Fax 020 7581 8115
www.tylerlondon.com
Page 9br

Voon Wong & Benson Saw
Unit 27, 1 Stannary Street
London SE11 4AD
020 7587 0116
Fax 020 7840 0178
www.voon-benson.co.uk
Pages 2, 82–83, 126–127, 132r

William W. Stubbs, IIDA
William W. Stubbs and
Associates
2100 Tanglewilde, Suite 17
Houston, TX 77063
stubbsww1@aol.com
Page 9br

Zynk Design Consultants
11 The Chandlery
50 Westminster Bridge Road
London SE1 7QY
020 7721 7444
Fax 020 7721 7443
www.zynkdesign.com
Page 104ar

PHOTOGRAPHY

KEY: *ph*= photographer, **a**=above, **b**=below, **r**=right, **l**=left, **c**=centre.

Endpapers *ph* Chris Everard/interior designer Angela Kearsey's house in London—architectural design by Dols Wong Architects, interior design by Angela Kearsey; **page 1** *ph* Andrew Wood/Paula Pryke and Peter Romaniuk's house in London; **2** *ph* Jan Baldwin/the Campbell family's apartment in London, architecture by Voon Wong Architects; **3** *ph* Debi Treloar/Julia and David O'Driscoll's house in London; **4–5** *ph* Chris Everard/Mark Weinstein's apartment in New York designed by Lloyd Schwan; **6** *ph* Dan Duchars/designer Mark Smith's home in London; **7** *ph* Debi Treloar/an apartment in London by Malin Iovino Design; **8l** *ph* Dan Duchars/designer Mark Smith's home in London; **8r** *ph* Debi Treloar/Mark and Sally of Baileys Home and Garden's house in Herefordshire; **9a** *ph* Chris Everard/Jo Warman—Interior Concepts; **9bl** *ph* Polly Wreford/Francesca Mills' house in London; **9br** *ph* Christopher Drake/a house in London, architectural design and procurement by Tyler London Ltd, interior design by William W. Stubbs, IIDA; **10 background** *ph* Polly Wreford/Marie-Hélène de Taillac's pied-à-terre in Paris; **10 inset** *ph* Debi Treloar/Catherine Chermayeff and Jonathan David's family home in New York designed by Asfour Guzy Architects; **10–11** *ph* Debi Treloar/family home, Bankside, London; **11** *ph* Debi Treloar/Kristiina Ratia and Jeff Gocke's family home in Norwalk, Connecticut; **12** *ph* Chris Everard/designed by Mullman Seidman Architects; **12–13** *ph* Chris Everard/an apartment in Paris designed by architects Guillaume Terver and Fabienne Couvert of cxt sarl d'architecture; **13** *ph* Jan Baldwin/a house in Maine designed by Stephen Blatt Architects; **14** *ph* Debi Treloar/Wim and Josephine's apartment in Amsterdam; **14–15** *ph* Debi Treloar/the designer couple Tea Bendix and Tobias Jacobsen's home, Denmark; **15** *ph* Debi Treloar/Mark Chalmers' apartment in Amsterdam; **16–17** *ph* Chris Everard/Central Park West Residence, New York City designed by Bruce Bierman Design, Inc.; **18l** *ph* Chris Everard/John Barman's Park Avenue apartment; **18r** *ph* Andrew Wood/a house in London designed by Bowles and Linares; **18–19** *ph* Jan Baldwin/Jan Hashey and Yasuo Minagawa; **19 both insets** *ph* Chris Everard/an apartment in Paris designed by architect Paul Collier; **20a** *ph* Chris Everard/photographer Guy Hills' house in London designed by Joanna Rippon and Maria Speake of Retrouvius; **20b** *ph* Jan Baldwin; **21al & 21 inset** *ph* Chris Everard/designed by Mullman Seidman Architects; **21 background** *ph* Debi Treloar/Kristiina Ratia and Jeff Gocke's family home in Norwalk, Connecticut; **22** *ph* Chris Everard/John Harman's apartment in London designed by Granit Chartered Architects; **23a** *ph* Debi Treloar/Robert Elms and Christina Wilson's family home in London; **23b** *ph* Andrew Wood/architect Grethe Meyer's house, Hørsholm, Denmark, built by architects Moldenhawer, Hammer and Frederiksen, 1963; **24a** *ph* Alan Williams/private apartment in London designed by Hugh Broughton Architects; **24b** Christopher Drake/owner Monique Davidson's family home in Normandy; **24–25** *ph* Debi Treloar/family home, Bankside, London; **25a** *ph* Debi Treloar/Cristine Tholstrup Hermansen and Helge Drenck's house in Copenhagen; **25b** *ph* Chris Everard/a house in London designed by Helen Ellery of The Plot London; **26l** *ph* Jan Baldwin/the Fitzwilliam-Lay's family home—architecture by Totem Design, interior design by Henri Fitzwilliam-Lay and Totem Design; **26r** *ph* Jan Baldwin/Sophie Eadie's family home in London; **27l** *ph* Debi Treloar/Catherine Chermayeff and Jonathan David's family home in New York designed by Asfour Guzy Architects; **27r** *ph* Jan Baldwin/the owner of Tessuti, Catherine Vindevogel-Debal's house in Kortrijk, Belgium, kitchen designed by Filip Van Bever; **28al** *ph* Chris Everard/an apartment in Milan designed by Nicoletta Marazza; **28bl** *ph* Debi Treloar/Mark Chalmers' apartment in Amsterdam; **28r** *ph* Catherine Gratwicke/Lesley Dilcock's house in London; **29l** *ph* Christopher Drake/Fiona and Woody Woodhouse's 16th-century weatherboard cottage in Surrey designed by Bexon Woodhouse Creative; **29r** *ph* Debi Treloar/Cristine Tholstrup Hermansen and Helge Drenck's house in Copenhagen; **30a** *ph* Dan Duchars/architects Patrick Theis and Soraya Khan's home in London; **30b & 31br** *ph* Debi Treloar/the home of Patty Collister in London, owner of An Angel At My Table; **31l** *ph* Andrew Wood/architect Grethe Meyer's house, Hørsholm, Denmark, built by architects Moldenhawer, Hammer and Frederiksen, 1963; **31ar** *ph* Dan Duchars/designer Mark Smith's home in London; **32–33** *ph* Chris Everard/Michael Nathenson's house in London; **34al** *ph* Chris Everard/an apartment in Milan designed by Tito Canella of Canella & Achilli Architects; **34ar** *ph* Debi Treloar/new-build house in Notting Hill designed by Seth Stein Architects; **34b** *ph* Andrew Wood/architect Grethe Meyer's house, Hørsholm, Denmark, built by architects Moldenhawer, Hammer and Frederiksen, 1963; **35** *ph* Chris Everard/architect Jonathan Clark's home in London; **36al** Chris Everard/Mark Weinstein's apartment in New York designed by Lloyd Schwan; **36ar** *ph* Debi Treloar/a family home in Manhattan designed by architect Amanda Martocchio and Gustavo Martinez Design; **36c & 36b** *ph* Debi Treloar/the home of Patty Collister in London, owner of An Angel At My Table; **37** *ph* Jan Baldwin/Claire Haithwaite and Dean Maryon's home in Amsterdam; **38al & ar** *ph* Jan Baldwin/Alfredo Paredes and Brad Goldfarb's loft in Tribeca, New York designed by Michael Neumann Architecture; **38bl** *ph* Chris Everard/a house in London designed by Helen Ellery of The Plot London; **38br** *ph* Debi Treloar/Sarah Munro and Brian Ayling's home in London; **39** *ph* Polly Wreford/Robert Merrett and Luis Peral's apartment in London; **40l** *ph* Chris Everard/Yuen-Wei Chew's apartment in London designed by Paul Daly Design Studio Ltd; **40ar** *ph* Debi Treloar/Catherine Chermayeff and Jonathan David's family home in New York designed by Asfour Guzy Architects; **40br** *ph* Chris Everard/apartment of Amy Harte Hossfeld and Martin Hossfeld; **41 both** *ph* Dan Duchars/architect Haifa Hammami's home in London; **42** *ph* Chris Everard/François Muracciole's apartment in Paris; **43 both** *ph* Jan Baldwin/Wendy Jansen and Chris Van Eldik, owners of J.O.B. Interieur's house in Wijk bij Duurstede, The Netherlands; **44** *ph* Chris Everard/Signora Venturini's apartment in Milan; **45l** *ph* Debi Treloar/Clare and David Mannix-Andrews' house, Hove, East Sussex; **45r** *ph* Debi Treloar/Kate and Dominic Ash's home in London; **46a** *ph* Chris Everard/Signora Venturini's apartment in Milan; **46b** *ph* Polly Wreford/an apartment in New York designed by Belmont Freeman Architects; **47a both** *ph* Chris Everard/Charles Bateson's house in London; **47b** *ph* Dan Duchars/Ian Hogarth of Hogarth Architects' home in London; **48–49** *ph* Chris Everard/Jo Warman—Interior Concepts; **50–51** *ph* Debi Treloar/a family home in London; **51 both** *ph* Chris Everard/designed by Mullman Seidman Architects; **52** *ph* Jan Baldwin/the Fitzwilliam-Lay's family home—architecture by Totem Design, interior design by Henri Fitzwilliam-Lay and Totem Design; **53** *ph* Chris Everard/the loft of Mary and Sean Kelly designed by Steven Learner Studio; **54** *ph* Chris Everard/architect Jonathan Clark's home in London; **55** *ph* Chris Everard/Jo Warman—Interior Concepts; **56a** *ph* Chris Everard/Michael Nathenson's house in London; **56b** *ph* Andrew Wood/Jamie Falla and Lynn Graham's house in London; **57a** *ph* Chris Everard/interior designer Angela Kearsey's house in London—architectural design by Dols Wong Architects, interior design by Angela Kearsey; **57bl** *ph* Debi Treloar; **57br** *ph* Debi Treloar/Catherine Chermayeff and Jonathan David's family home in New York designed by Asfour Guzy Architects; **58–59** *ph* Dan Duchars/Ian Hogarth of Hogarth Architects' home office in London; **60** *ph* Chris Everard/an apartment in New York designed by Mullman Seidman Architects; **61l** *ph* Debi Treloar/Robert Elms and Christina Wilson's family home in London; **61r** *ph* Chris Everard/Yuen-Wei Chew's apartment in London designed by Paul Daly Design Studio Ltd; **62** *ph* Andrew Wood/Chelsea Studio New York City designed by Marino and Giolito; **63 & 64** *ph* Debi Treloar/Catherine Chermayeff and Jonathan David's family home in New York designed by Asfour Guzy Architects; **65** *ph* Dan Duchars/architect Haifa Hammami's home in London; **66 both** *ph* Polly Wreford/Lena Proudlock's home Gloucestershire has since been restyled; **66–67** *ph* Polly Wreford/Marie-Hélène de Taillac's pied-à-terre in Paris; **68l** *ph* Dan Duchars/designer Mark

Smith's home in London; **68r** *ph* Polly Wreford/Clare Nash's former home in London; **69** *ph* Dan Duchars/Ian Hogarth of Hogarth Architects' home office in London; **70al** *ph* Chris Everard/an apartment in Paris designed by architects Guillaume Terver and Fabienne Couvert of cxt sarl d'architecture; **70bl** *ph* Debi Treloar/Catherine Chermayeff and Jonathan David's family home in New York designed by Asfour Guzy Architects; **70–71a** *ph* Andrew Wood; **70–71b** *ph* Jan Baldwin/Alfredo Paredes and Brad Goldfarb's loft in Tribeca, New York designed by Michael Neumann Architecture; **71** *ph* Andrew Wood/a house in Stockholm, Sweden; **72–73** *ph* Dan Duchars/stylist Rose Hammick and architect Andrew Treverton's home in London; **74–75** *ph* Chris Everard/Central Park West residence, New York City designed by Bruce Bierman Design, Inc.; **76–77** *ph* Dan Duchars/architects Patrick Theis and Soraya Khan's home in London; **78–79** *ph* Dan Duchars/stylist Rose Hammick and architect Andrew Treverton's home in London; **80–81** *ph* James Merrell/an apartment in New York designed by Marino & Giolito; **81l** *ph* Andrew Wood/Anthony Swanson's apartment in London designed by Stickland Coombe; **81r** *ph* Andrew Wood; **82–83** *ph* Christopher Drake/Florence Lim's house in London—architecture by Voon Wong Architects, interior design by Florence Lim Design; **84** *ph* Christopher Drake/Clare Mosley's house in London; **85b both** *ph* Chris Everard/architect Jonathan Clark's home in London; **85a** *ph* Chris Everard/a house in London designed by Helen Ellery of The Plot London; **86–87** *ph* Chris Everard/the London apartment of the Sheppard Day Design Partnership; **87a** *ph* Debi Treloar/architect Simon Colebrook's home in London; **87b** *ph* Jan Baldwin/Sophie Eadie's family home in London; **88a** *ph* Catherine Gratwicke/Laura Stoddart's apartment in London; **88b** *ph* Chris Everard/Jo Warman—Interior Concepts; **89l** *ph* Chris Everard/Mark Weinstein's apartment in New York designed by Lloyd Schwan; **89ar** *ph* Catherine Gratwicke/designer Ann-Louise Roswald's apartment in London; **89br** *ph* Chris Everard/Ben Atfield's house in London; **90l** *ph* Catherine Gratwicke/Laura Stoddart's apartment in London; **90ar** *ph* Chris Everard/Lisa and Richard Frisch's apartment in New York designed by Patricia Seidman of Mullman Seidman Architects; **90br** *ph* Andrew Wood/a house in London designed by Guy Stansfeld 020 8962 8666; **91** *ph* Polly Wreford/Clare Nash's former home in London; **92** *ph* Debi Treloar/family home, Bankside, London; **93l** *ph* Chris Everard/apartment of Amy Harte Hossfeld and Martin Hossfeld; **93c** *ph* Chris Everard/Mark Weinstein's apartment in New York designed by Lloyd Schwan; **93r** *ph* Chris Everard/John Harman's apartment in London designed by Granit Chartered Architects; **94** *ph* Chris Everard/Bob and Maureen Macris' apartment on Fifth Avenue in New York designed by Sage Wimer Coombe Architects; **94–95** *ph* Dan Duchars/architect Haifa Hammami's home in London; **95 & 96al** *ph* Dan Duchars/designer Mark Smith's home in London; **96ar** *ph* Debi Treloar/Susan Cropper's family home in London—www.63hlg.com; **96b** *ph* Chris Everard/Yuen-Wei Chew's apartment in London designed by Paul Daly Design Studio Ltd; **97a** *ph* Chris Everard/an apartment in Paris designed by architects Guillaume Terver and Fabienne Couvert of cxt sarl d'architecture; **96b** *ph* Polly Wreford; **98–99** *ph* Christopher Drake/a house designed by artist Angela A'Court; **100 main** *ph* Jan Baldwin/a house in New York designed by Brendan Coburn and Joseph Smith of Coburn Architecture; **100 inset** *ph* Debi Treloar/Catherine Chermayeff and Jonathan David's family home in New York designed by Asfour Guzy Architects; **101a** *ph* Debi Treloar/Nicky Phillips' apartment in London; **101b** *ph* Debi Treloar/Robert Elms and Christina Wilson's family home in London; **102** *ph* Debi Treloar/Susan Cropper's family home in London—www.63hlg.com; **103l** *ph* Chris Everard/Hilton McConnico's house near Paris; **103r** *ph* Debi Treloar/family home, Bankside, London; **104l** *ph* Debi Treloar/Clare and David Mannix-Andrews' house, Hove, East Sussex; **104ar** *ph* Chris Everard/designed by Zynk Design Consultants, One New Inn Square, a private dining room and home of chef David Vanderhook, all enquiries 020 7729 3645; **104bl** *ph* Debi Treloar; **105** *ph* Debi Treloar/Susan Cropper's family home in London—www.63hlg.com; **106** *ph* Jan Baldwin/Wendy Jansen and Chris Van Eldik, owners of J.O.B. Interieur's house in Wijk bij Duurstede, The Netherlands; **107l** *ph* Chris Everard/the Sugarman–Behun house on Long Island; **107r** *ph* Chris Everard/Richard Hopkin's apartment in London designed by HM2; **108l** *ph* Chris Everard/Monique Witt and Steven Rosenblum's apartment in New York, designed by Mullman Seidman Architects; **108r** *ph* Chris Everard/architect Nigel Smith's apartment in London; **108–109** *ph* Jan Baldwin/Sophie Eadie's family home in London; **109l** *ph* Chris Everard/a house in Hampstead, London designed by Orefelt Associates; **109r** *ph* Andrew Wood/Johanne Riss' house in Brussels; **110a** *ph* Jan Baldwin/Claire Haithwaite and Dean Maryon's home in Amsterdam; **110b** *ph* Chris Everard/Suze Orman's apartment in New York designed by Patricia Seidman of Mullman Seidman Architects; **111** *ph* Debi Treloar/Nicky Phillips' apartment in London; **112al** *ph* Debi Treloar/Ian Hogarth of Hogarth Architects' family home in London; **112ac** *ph* Chris Everard; **112bl** *ph* Andrew Wood/Roger Oates and Fay Morgan's house in Eastnor; **112r** *ph* Debi Treloar/Mark and Sally of Baileys Home and Garden's house in Herefordshire; **113a** *ph* Dan Duchars/stylist Rose Hammick and architect Andrew Treverton's home in London; **113bl** *ph* Jan Baldwin; **113br** *ph* Jan Baldwin/a house in New York designed by Brendan Coburn and Joseph Smith of Coburn Architecture; **114–115** *ph* Debi Treloar/Victoria Andreae's house in London; **116** *ph* Debi Treloar/Elizabeth Alford and Michael Young's loft in New York; **117a** *ph* Debi Treloar/Ian Hogarth of Hogarth Architects' family home in London; **117b** *ph* Debi Treloar/Julia and David O'Driscoll's house in London; **118al** *ph* Debi Treloar/family home, Bankside, London; **118ar** *ph* Debi Treloar/Ben Johns and Deb Waterman Johns' house in Georgetown; **118b** *ph* Debi Treloar/Kate and Dominic Ash's home in London; **119** *ph* Dan Duchars/architects Patrick Theis and Soraya Khan's home in London; **120** *ph* Debi Treloar/new-build house in Notting Hill designed by Seth Stein Architects; **121** *ph* Debi Treloar/Robert Elms and Christina Wilson's family home in London; **122l** *ph* Debi Treloar/Eben and Nica Cooper's bedroom, the Cooper family playroom; **122–123 & 123l** *ph* Debi Treloar/the Boyes' home in London designed by Circus Architects; **123r** *ph* Debi Treloar/new-build house in Notting Hill designed by Seth Stein Architects; **124a** *ph* Debi Treloar/Catherine Chermayeff and Jonathan David's family home in New York designed by Asfour Guzy Architects; **124b** *ph* Debi Treloar/Julia and David O'Driscoll's house in London; **125** *ph* Debi Treloar/a family home in London; **126–127** *ph* Jan Baldwin/the Campbell family's apartment in London, architecture by Voon Wong Architects; **128l** *ph* Chris Everard/interior designer Angela Kearsey's house in London—architectural design by Dols Wong Architects, interior design by Angela Kearsey; **128–129** *ph* Andrew Wood/Charlotte Crosland's home in London, designed by Charlotte Crosland Interiors; **129l** *ph* Chris Everard/an actor's London home designed by Site Specific; **129r** *ph* Chris Everard/an apartment in Milan designed by Tito Canella of Canella & Achilli Architects; **130 & 131al** *ph* Christopher Drake/Andrea Spencer's house in London; **131ar** *ph* Christopher Drake/Dick and Vanessa Cooper's house in London designed by Eger Architects; **131b** *ph* Andrew Wood/Charlotte Crosland's home in London designed by Charlotte Crosland Interiors; **132l** *ph* Christopher Drake/Barbara Benenson Warren and Marc Warren's apartment in New York designed by Scott Specht and Louise Harpman; **132r** *ph* Christopher Drake/Florence Lim's house in London—architecture by Voon Wong Architects, interior design by Florence Lim Design; **133** *ph* Simon Upton; **134–135** *ph* Debi Treloar/designed by Sage Wimer Coombe Architects; **135l** *ph* James Merrell; **135r** *ph* Chris Everard/Mark Kirkley and Harumi Kaijima's house in Sussex; **136** *ph* Christopher Drake/Jonathan and Camilla Ross's house in London; **136–137** *ph* Andrew Wood/Roger and Suzy Black's apartment in London designed by Johnson Naylor; **137** *ph* Christopher Drake/Andrea Spencer's house in London.

INDEX

Page numbers in *italics*
refer to illustrations.